THE EFFECTIVE
ELEMENTARY CLASSROOM

Managing for Success

Geoffrey Colvin
Mike Lazar

94ELEM/9-03/C&M/750/268

Edited by Lynne Timmons
Text layout and cover design by Susan Fogo
Cover photo: Images © 1997 PhotoDisc, Inc.

Printed in the United States of America
Published and Distributed by:

SOPRIS
WEST
EDUCATIONAL SERVICES

4093 Specialty Place Longmont, Colorado 80504
(303) 651-2829 www.sopriswest.com

Geoffrey Colvin, Ph.D. is a nationally recognized educational consultant to school districts and agencies on the best instruction and behavior management practices to use with the full range of student needs. He draws directly on his extensive experiences as a certified teacher in both general and special education. He directed a county-wide school for seriously emotionally disturbed youth and administered a juvenile detention school for five years. He has authored and co-authored over sixty publications on the subject of teaching and managing problem behavior including a very popular text, *Antisocial Behavior in Schools: Strategies and Best Practices*. Currently, Dr. Colvin is a research associate at the University of Oregon.

Mike Lazar, M.Ed. is a highly respected teacher with 23 years of direct classroom experience. He has taught students at all elementary grade levels and has served as a Mentor Teacher with the University of Oregon Resident Teacher Program. He has held several leadership and consultant positions related to curriculum development and implementation including consultant for Sunburst Communication Software Curriculum Planner. He is highly regarded for his classroom organization and effective teaching practices. He has served as head teacher and currently teaches third grade at Hillside Elementary School in Eugene, Oregon.

Dedication

Dedicated to our Families
Nola and Kylee
&
Carol, Kelly, Carrie, and Cindy

Acknowledgments

Thanks are due to the following for their peer reviews and constructive feedback: Sharyn Shaw, Jerrlyn Henery, Randy Sprick, Tim Lewis, Stu Greenberg, Pat Mullen, Ben Baker, and Mary Rosenbaum.

Contents

Introduction

CLASSROOM TEACHING HAS been described as one of the most complex professions of the day. Teachers not only have to manage a wide variety of responsibilities, but they have to be able to orchestrate multiple activities at the same time. Teachers can easily become overwhelmed with the task and find that they spend more and more time trying to manage these multiple responsibilities and less time on actual teaching.

This book will assist elementary teachers, K-5, with organizing and managing their classroom. There are two basic emphases here. First is a careful description of the preparation and planning steps for organizing an elementary classroom. These steps are based on common, successful practices and research applications designed for elementary classrooms. The assumption is that if the teacher is well prepared and the classroom is well organized, many problems can be prevented, responsibilities can be managed in a timely manner, and the teacher will more likely be successful. Second, student behavior, such as classroom expectations and classroom routines, needs to be systematically taught. This is accomplished using the standard instructional procedures that are used to teach skills in other areas such as academics or sports. The bottom line is, if teachers want certain behaviors from their students, they need to provide instruction on these behaviors. That is, they need to provide steps to ensure that their students understand what is required, have structured occasions to practice these expected behaviors with adequate monitoring and feedback, and have opportunities to exhibit the behaviors independently. This book outlines specific methods for teaching all aspects of behavioral expectations.

Several organizational and planning variables are addressed in this user-friendly format, including arranging the classroom, developing schedules, and grouping students. Other chapters focus on teaching behavior: establishing classroom expectations and routines, and preventing and managing problem behavior. The final chapters discuss working with other key personnel and getting ready for the school year.

There are several groups of teachers who will profit from the topics in this book. First is the beginning teacher. These teachers, in many cases, do not get adequate training on the concrete details for establishing and maintaining an effective classroom. Unfortunately, they are expected to learn this information once they begin teaching. Second, there are teachers who may have been struggling for a few years because they have not learned these details. Third, some teachers may have been relatively successful with the way they have managed their classrooms in earlier years of their career. However, more recently they may have had changes in their school population and their methods have been less successful. Finally, a successful teacher may read this book with the notion that, "Here is an idea I can use." Or, experienced teachers may be reminded of procedures that are effective and that they have omitted over time.

The first day of a new school year always presents challenges, both to new and seasoned teachers. The ideas presented in this book will help teachers get organized, stay organized, and be prepared for situations as they arise. A well-organized classroom provides students with a proactive and predictable environment necessary for behavior control and quality learning to take place. The effort applied at the beginning of the school year will pay off handsomely long after classes are in full swing, in terms of happier, more manageable students—and more satisfied, effective teachers, too.

> Developing
> Classroom Structure

CLASSROOM STRUCTURE IS a general term used to describe the manner in which teachers organize their classroom. The overall goal of establishing structure is to ensure that activities in the classroom are as predictable as possible. In this way, the activities are more likely to make sense to the students and increase the chance that the social and academic learning goals will be achieved. In addition it is well established that students who exhibit problem behavior are more likely to be successful in classrooms that are well organized and have an adequate level of structure. This can be accomplished by: (1) Organizing the classroom space; (2) Developing a classroom schedule; and (3) Establishing classroom expectations.

Organizing the Classroom Space

Many different functions take place in the classroom on a regular basis, and the success or failure of these functions will depend on the way in which the classroom is designed. To organize the classroom space, first clearly identify all functions and activities necessary for instruction, and then carefully arrange the room to accomplish these functions. Suggested functions and corresponding classroom design are:

Independent work requires an area with minimum distraction. It is best for individual desks to separate students. Independent work areas should be in a low traffic section away from materials, time out areas, and free activity areas.

Group work areas must be structured so that students can attend to the teacher and to each other. Groups should be located in an area that enhances instruction and minimizes distraction; situate the groups toward the front of the class. The teacher, too, is normally in front of the groups to ensure supervision. Seating arrangements can also enhance group instruction. Common arrangements used are semicircles, rows, and small clusters.

Choice activity is available sometimes for students who finish their work early or as a reward for special achievement. Restrict this activity to a quiet location behind the instructional areas. Specific rules of behavior also should be in place and enforced to lessen distraction.

Time out or penalty area is used as a negative consequence in the classroom for students whose behavior is unacceptable. This area could consist of a desk in the corner of the room, a small table facing the back of the room, or a desk at the side of the classroom. This consequence also serves as a signal to all students that the behavior is not acceptable in the classroom.

Select an area that isolates the student from the other students to limit their interactions. If more than one student is isolated at one time, they need to be separated.

Quiet time area is used by some teachers to enable a student to calm down for whatever reason. This area needs to be as isolated as possible to prevent interactions with other students and staff.

Teacher's desk is placed out of the way and receives as little use as possible during instruction. Locate the desk in a near-zero traffic area to safeguard personal property and confidential material. This area should be as secure as possible. Locate the desk in a corner away from the door. Lock the desk when it is not being used.

Storage materials are located in low-traffic areas to avoid distraction and allow easy access. Ensure that materials are neatly arranged and that they don't obstruct supervision. Do not store materials in high places. Ensure there is free access to the door in case of emergencies.

Notice board is placed in an area that is highly visible, high-traffic, and does not divert student attention during instruction. Divide the notice board into sections for specific communication such as news, special projects, and rules.

The seating arrangement can vary considerably. The key is flexibility. Remember, too, that *supervision* is maximized by arranging the room so that all students are in sight. Be careful of high objects, such as book shelves, that may obstruct supervision.

Use the following guidelines in developing a seating plan (given there is sufficient space):

1. Ensure all students can easily see presentations during whole group instruction.

2. Minimize distractions.

3. Use clusters for small group instruction, generally 4-5 students per group.

4. Change the seating chart periodically so that students are placed next to different students.

5. Involve the students in the seating plans as appropriate. Students' choice of seating could be used as a reward for students who have met a predetermined criteria. However, the teacher reserves the right to determine the seating arrangements.

6. Vary the seating arrangement periodically (rows, semicircular arrangements, and clusters).

Three typical classroom arrangements are:

- Whole class instruction
- Small group activities
- Small group instruction combined with independent work

Examples of these arrangements are shown in Figure 1.

FIGURE 1: Examples of Classroom Arrangements

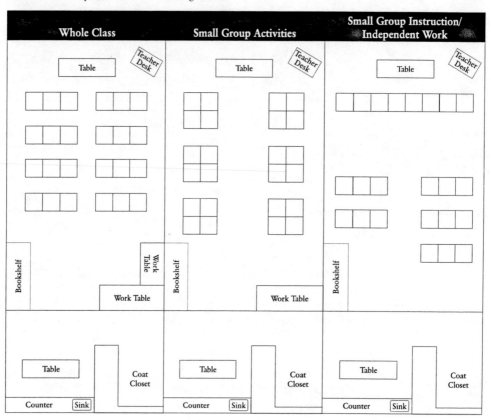

Developing a Classroom Schedule

Perhaps no other variable contributes more to establishing classroom structure than the classroom schedule. The schedule provides for the organization of all the classroom activities and school events. It also provides the basis for establishing a stable, predictable environment for learning. Teachers must not only develop a schedule very carefully, but they should consistently follow the schedule.

Unfortunately, the teacher is somewhat limited in developing a schedule. The reason is that the classroom schedule has to be coordinated with the school-wide schedules such as lunch and recess, as well as with other teachers, specialist teachers, and other events. To develop a schedule the following steps are recommended:

Steps in Developing a Classroom Schedule

STEP ONE
School-Wide Schedule

Make a list of all school-wide events that have fixed schedules (e.g., lunch and recess). These events typically include:

- The start of the school day
- Pledge and school announcements
- Recess
- Lunch
- End of school day
- Special events such as school assemblies

STEP TWO
Specialists' Schedule

List the predetermined periods allocated to specialist teachers. These teachers
have limited flexibility because of room stipulations. For example, the music
teacher conducts music in the music room, which is scheduled for use
throughout the day. Consequently, rescheduling one teacher's class will likely
affect another teacher's class. Specialist schedules usually include:

- Music
- Art
- Physical education
- Library, media center, or computer laboratory

> *Note:* If classroom teachers are expected to teach these content areas, schedule
> these subjects within your own classroom timetable. In addition, the schedule for
> special education students and title (educationally disadvantaged students who
> qualify for instructional assistance) students who receive instruction outside the
> classroom will need to be incorporated in the classroom schedule.

STEP THREE
Team Teaching

If some subjects are taught on a team teaching basis, plan the schedule with
participating teachers. A particular time slot is agreed upon, such as the first
45 minutes after recess. This time slot becomes fixed so that the teacher builds
the individual classroom schedule around this period.

STEP FOUR
Order of Subjects

Once the fixed scheduled events have been identified, you can schedule the
classroom subjects and activities. However, give careful attention to the order
of these subjects. For example, the basic academic skills—reading, writing,
math, and spelling—should be scheduled as early in the day as possible.

The Effective Elementary Classroom

Students are typically fresher and more cooperative at this time, and these subjects are essential for the students' success in school. In general, prioritize the subjects and activities to be conducted in your classroom.

STEP FIVE
Master Schedule

Develop the master classroom schedule after all school-wide schedules have been determined and subjects and activities to be conducted in the classroom have been prioritized. Construct a master classroom schedule for the term to include periods for the major content areas within the classroom, school-wide programs, and specialist subjects. The master schedule will vary from day to day to accommodate specialist subjects, but try to ensure that the schedule is stable on a weekly basis. For example, just as music may be taught on Mondays, and physical education may be taught on Tuesdays and Fridays, so should basic skill subjects be scheduled for fixed times each day.

Also, use the master schedule as a basis to develop other schedules (first day, first few days, first week, and first month). A sample master classroom schedule is presented in Table 1 showing how the other schedules are developed from the master schedule.

The Effective Elementary Classroom

TABLE 1: Master Classroom Schedule, First Three Days

MASTER SCHEDULE	First Day	Second Day	Third Day
8:30-9:00 Spelling	Go over classroom rules/expectations. Practice Spelling System	Practice Spelling System	Practice Spelling System
9:00-9:45 Math	Testing	Testing	Testing
9:45-10:00 Recess	Practice lining up before going to recess	Practice lining up before going to recess	Practice lining up before going to recess
10:00-10:15 Story			
10:15-10:45 Social Studies/Science	Hand out text and materials, do overview	Begin Unit	Begin Unit
10:45-11:25 Reading	Testing	Testing	Testing
11:25-11:50 Language Arts	Hand out text and materials, do overview	Begin Unit	Begin Unit
11:50-12:35 Lunch	Practice getting ready and lining up before lunch	Practice getting ready and lining up before lunch	Practice getting ready and lining up before lunch
12:40-1:00 Story			
1:00-1:30 Computers/P.E.	Review hall behavior before going to Computers/P.E.	Review hall behavior before going to Computers/P.E.	Review hall behavior before going to Computers/P.E.
1:30-2:00 Penmanship	Hand out materials, begin lessons	Continue lessons	Continue lessons
2:00-2:25 S.S.R., silent reading	Go over expectations of silent reading	Review expectations	Review expectations

STEP SIX
Schedules for the First Day, First Few Days, First Week, and First Month of School

Within this master schedule develop schedules to carry you through the first full month of school. It is very important that the beginning of the school year goes well for the students. A strong positive start sets the tone for the year.

  The Effective Elementary Classroom

Schedule for the First Day—The primary emphasis for the first day is orientation. The main activities center on:

- Making the students welcome
- Teaching the class behavioral expectations
- Establishing the critical class routines
- Providing an overview of the class content and activities
- Explaining the use of the classroom and the building
- Motivating the students to have a great year

Build the specific first day activities into the master schedule. For example, take part of the reading period to teach the classroom behavioral expectations. A sample schedule for the first day is presented in the second column of Table 1, showing the relationship between the first day of school and the master schedule.

Schedule for the First Three Days—There is much information to be communicated to the students at the start of the school year. To avoid giving the students an "overdose" of information and to keep them from being too passive (sitting there listening to information for a greater part of their time), spread the critical information and activities over the first three days of the master schedule. Use these days to:

- Complete testing for student groupings where appropriate
- Teach and practice routines
- Teach and practice classroom behavioral expectations
- Give orientation for specialist classes and school-wide events
- Review content in major subject areas

An example of a schedule for the first three days is presented in Table 1. Note how the various activities are built into the master schedule.

Schedule for the First Full Week and First Month—At the close of the first week, begin to phase into the master schedule that should be operating for the first full week of school. Use this schedule to complete testing or any leftover tasks from the first few days of school. Develop the schedule for the first month so that the master schedule is implemented the remainder of the month. An example of a schedule for the first full week and first month is presented in Table 2.

TABLE 2:Master Schedule, First Full Week and First Month

MASTER SCHEDULE	First Full Week	First Month
8:30-9:00 Spelling	Start Spelling Units	Continue Units
9:00-9:45 Math	Put students into groups if necessary and begin first unit	Continue Units
9:45-10:00 Recess	Observe and give feedback on lining up for recess	Observe and give feedback weekly or when necessary
10:00-10:15 Story		
10:15-10:45 Social Studies/Science	Continue Units	Continue Units
10:45-11:25 Reading	Put students into groups if necessary and begin first unit	Continue Units
11:25-11:50 Language Arts	Continue Units	Continue Units
11:50-12:35 Lunch	Observe and give feedback on getting ready and lining up for recess	Observe and give feedback weekly or when necessary
12:40-1:00 Story		
1:00-1:30 Computers/P.E.	Observe and give feedback of hall behavior to and from Computer/P.E.	Observe and give feedback weekly or when necessary
1:30-2:00 Penmanship	Continue Lessons	Continue Lessons
2:00-2:25 S.S.R., silent reading	Observe and give feedback of behavior during silent reading.	Observe and give feedback weekly

S T E P   S E V E N
Schedule Review

Evaluate the schedule on a periodic basis, especially at the end of the first month. It is necessary to keep the schedule as stable as possible, but there may need to be some adjustments made once the year gets underway. It could be that certain subjects are not getting enough time, some subjects may be getting too much time, or the ordering may need to be changed as the students may be involved in too much movement. Review the schedule at the end of the first month and then at the end of each term or major cycle.

The Effective Elementary Classroom

Establishing Classroom Expectations

One of the most important tasks for the classroom teacher is to establish classroom expectations. If the expectations are effectively established, a positive classroom climate will result, enabling the teacher and the students to achieve their goals. It is the expectations that set the tone of the classroom, helping each student feel comfortable and safe, and maximizing learning. There are three steps in establishing classroom expectations: (1) Identify the expectations; (2) Plan for teaching the expectations; and (3) Develop procedures for systematically teaching these behaviors.

Identifying Classroom Behavioral Expectations

Classroom expectations are designed to provide students with clear information, in the form of rules, on the kinds of responses required of them so that instruction and learning take place. Following are several steps that facilitate teaching this relationship:

State the rules in a concrete form so it is clear to anyone (teacher, student or observer) when a rule has been kept or broken. For this reason, rules should be precise, practical, and expressed as concrete actions. Display the rules on a poster and number each rule.

Select functional rules that focus on student behaviors that facilitate instruction and learning. Choose rules that readily generate positive and negative examples. Teachers may introduce more specific rules as needed. Remember to review and revise the rules throughout the school year.

Some examples of classroom expectations are:

1. Follow directions quickly.

2. Pay attention and join in class activities.

3. Respect each other's space.

4. Raise your hand to speak.

5. Stay in your seat or assigned area.

Planning to Teach Classroom Expectations

Develop a plan to actively teach the behavioral expectations. Do not assume that telling or posting the rules will be sufficient. Use the following steps to teach the behavioral expectations.

Teach the rules immediately on the first day of the new school year because any "down time" usually makes it more difficult to establish the rules.

Some teachers prefer to involve the students in the development of these expectations. In these cases you should have an outline of expectations and some clarification of what you expect.

Rehearse and review the rules regularly throughout the first month of school so students are constantly reminded of the rules. In this way you, as well as the students, can identify which rules are not working or need further clarification.

Practice the rules and the consequences of breaking them by simulating situations. For example, if the students are too noisy coming in from recess, have the students leave the room, wait in the hallway, line up, and come into the room quietly.

Use positive reinforcement for students who demonstrate expected behavior (see Chapter 5).

Teaching Classroom Expectations

View classroom expectations as a set of skills that need to be taught to the students. Apply the same teaching principles and strategies employed to establish academic, sport, and social skills to teaching classroom behavior. Essentially, if you want the students to exhibit certain behaviors, you need to teach these behaviors using the same instructional procedures you would use to teach academic skills. Typically, teachers use five steps to teach a skill: (1) Explain; (2) Specify student behaviors; (3) Practice; (4) Monitor; and (5) Review.

STEP ONE
Explain

Give the students adequate reasons and purposes for the particular behavior. Make sure that the students understand what you require of them and why you require it. Encourage the students to discuss the rules and why they are needed, ask questions, and develop strategies. Get the students involved in the development of strategies to ensure understanding and to facilitate cooperation. At the close of the discussion, ask questions related to the purpose of the rules and the specific behavior that will be expected. Student responses will indicate their level of understanding.

STEP TWO
Specify Student Behaviors

Clearly specify the behaviors that are required of the students. These behaviors should be discrete, sequential, and observable. For example, if you expect the students to cooperate, you could ask the students to open their math books to page 54. The students who get out their books and open them to page 54 within a few seconds would be demonstrating the behavior of cooperation. On the other hand, the students who do not open their books to page 54 or who take several minutes to complete the task would not be showing cooperation. The level of detail and order often varies from class to class and from teacher to teacher. Establish sufficient detail in the behaviors to ensure that the purpose of the routine is accomplished.

STEP THREE
Practice

Teachers typically use practice to develop fluency in skill development. Likewise, you should schedule practice sessions to develop behavior expectations. Model the first example of the skill to ensure that the students observe a correct example. Next, call upon the students to role play. Use small groups of students to demonstrate the routine. Make sure all students have an opportunity to demonstrate and practice the expected behavior. Do not require the students to behave properly in the real situation until they have demonstrated proficiency in the practice sessions.

S T E P   F O U R
Monitor

Once the students have had the opportunity to practice the expected behavior, the next step is to provide them with opportunities to demonstrate the behaviors independently in real situations. Carefully monitor the students' performance, especially in the early stages. Catch problems early, provide praise or reinforcement to students who demonstrate the expected behaviors correctly, and provide prompts, correction, and encouragement to students who may be making errors. Provide feedback to the students on their performance at the completion of the activity.

S T E P   F I V E
Review

Develop a system to periodically review the students' performance on the expected behaviors. Include formal observation of the students' behavior to assess: how many of the students are following the expected behaviors, how long the demonstrations are taking, and what kinds of errors are occurring. If errors occur, briefly introduce steps one, two, and three before the next opportunity to demonstrate the expected behaviors.

The five steps in developing an instruction plan to teach classroom expectations are illustrated in Table 3.

Note: More structure is usually needed for younger students, larger groups of students, and classes comprised of a large number of students with problem behaviors.

TABLE 3: Example of an Instruction Plan for Teaching a Classroom Expectation

Expected Behavior: Cooperate With Others
STEP ONE: Explain There are many students in your classroom. All need to cooperate so that each can learn, belong, and feel safe. Ask the students why it is necessary to cooperate with others. Ask them what happens when we cooperate with each other and what happens when we don't. Ask for some examples of cooperation and some examples that show lack of cooperation.

STEP TWO: Specify Student Behaviors
 	
To cooperate means to:
    1. Follow the teacher's directions
    2. Take a turn
    3. Share
    4. Work together when necessary
    5. Follow the classroom and school rules

STEP THREE: Practice Use three steps to provide practice: (1) Individual model: Model the behavior yourself, or select reliable students to model the behavior; (2) Small group model: Select a few students to model the behavior as a group and request the rest of the class to watch; and (3) Whole class practice: Conduct whole class responses. For example: *Individual Model*—Say, "I am going to show you what following directions looks like. First, Joe will be given a direction, then Selena." Ask Joe to open his math book to page 54. Identify the critical responses such as, "Notice how Joe stopped what he was doing, got out his book, opened it to page 54 quickly, and that was all he did." Present another direction to Selena: "Selena, put your books away and wait at the door please." *Small Group Model*—Say, "Now I am going to present some directions to Antonio, Mary, and Chu. I want everyone to watch them. Antonio, Mary, and Chu, put your books away please. Take out your math book and open it to page 21." Thank the students for following the directions and the rest of the class for watching. Comment on whether the students followed the directions quickly. Repeat this routine with other students.   (continued)

Whole Class Practice—Say, "Now it is everybody's turn. Listen for the direction, follow the direction quickly, and please do not do anything else. Put all your materials in your desk, and fold your arms on the desk." Provide feedback and conduct a brief discussion on how the class did. Present additional directions for further practice.

Conduct practice sessions for the other behaviors related to cooperation, take a turn, share, work together where necessary, and follow classroom and school rules.

STEP FOUR: Monitor

Now the students have an opportunity to demonstrate the expected behaviors during a natural setting. Monitor their performance by moving around and watching the students. For example, present the direction to put away the materials they are working on and get their math books out. Look around the whole classroom and acknowledge students who have started to put their materials away. For example, "I appreciate the students who have put their materials away already." Also, note the students who have not cooperated with the direction and prompt them. For example, "Some students have not started to put their materials away yet. Please hurry up."

STEP FIVE: Review

Provide the students with feedback on how they performed with the expected behavior. For example, if a high level of cooperation was obtained, "I am very pleased with the way the class cooperated with directions in this period. You followed the directions quickly. Thank you. Keep up the good work." If cooperation was not high, "We did not do very well with following directions this period. Some students did well. Thank you. But most of the class was too slow to follow the directions. I will remind you next period to try to be quicker. Let's see if we can improve."

Teaching classroom expectations is a critical step to establishing an effective classroom. Use the five steps of explain, specify the behaviors, practice, monitor, and review to develop instruction plans for each of the classroom expectations. Once the behaviors are established, be sure to follow up in a systematic manner to ensure that the students do not slip in their performance of these expectations.

Summary

Establishing a workable structure is the first step in setting up a classroom for success. The particular variables of importance are: (1) The design of the classroom space; (2) The schedule; and (3) The classroom expectations. Carefully review these three components before the students' first day of school, and systematically implement them throughout the entire school year.

| Establishing |
| Classroom Routines |

CLASSROOM ROUTINES REFER to those activities that are completed by students with minimum assistance from the teacher. Essentially, the goal is to have the students manage these tasks by themselves. The routines usually consist of a number of sequential behaviors to be managed independently by the students. For example, a teacher may expect the students to turn in completed assignments and products at a specific place in the room, return to their desk, and begin another activity without prompting from the teacher. This chapter describes six aspects of classroom routines: (1) Purpose and benefits; (2) Basic strategies for establishing the routines; (3) Common classroom routines; (4) Using routines to solve problems; (5) Checklists; and (6) Resources.

Purposes and Benefits of Classroom Routines

Develops Self-Management Skills

Teachers set self-management as a primary goal for their students. The more the students can do by themselves, the more likely they are to be responsible for their behavior both inside and outside the classroom. Self-management is a portable skill that transfers to less-supervised school settings such as recess, hallways, restrooms, and buses.

Provides Opportunities to Practice Skills

Practice is necessary for students to acquire fluency in skills. Teachers can provide their students with opportunities for practice as part of the classroom routines. For example, students could be directed to attempt a certain number of problems by themselves or work from examples in a textbook or worksheets. The teacher establishes expectations that students complete these examples by themselves. The routine would include procedures for securing help if needed and for ending the practice activity.

Serves Test or Diagnostic Purposes

One way of determining the class' mastery level of a skill or content is to establish a routine of independent practice. The teacher provides practice examples that are to be completed independently and turned in to the teacher in a designated manner. The students' performance on these examples provides the teacher with information on which students have mastered the skills and which students are still having problems. This helps the teacher to find error patterns and create strategies to correct the problems.

Manages "Administrivia" Efficiently

Typically, teachers have to manage many items related to schoolwide and district organization such as attendance, lunch choices, attendance at certain events, forms for immunization, and forms for school functions. These activities are called "Administrivia." They are tasks that need to be completed and often take a considerable amount of teacher time. Routines can be established where students take charge of these activities. The teacher describes the tasks to be done and develops a rotational system to place students in charge of collecting and delivering the required information. When students can take charge of these responsibilities, the teacher is freed to attend to other tasks and responsibilities.

Minimizes Disruptive Interactions

Some of the trends facing today's teachers are increases in class size, student heterogeneity and diversity with respect to ability, behavior, languages, and student needs. Some students become agitated when their needs are not met immediately. These students' behavior may escalate when there are high levels of student and teacher interactions. Classroom and independent routines help to provide a buffer for certain students. That is, students participate in activities that essentially help to minimize the number of disruptions.

Helps Create a Shared Ownership Between the Teacher and Students

Teachers are often concerned that some of their students do not care about their classroom because they exhibit behavior that they do not belong or want to belong. One way of connecting with these students is to involve them in the management of various routines. The more these students are called on to contribute to the planning and management of the classroom, the more they are likely to experience and express ownership. By involving the students in the development, implementation, and revision of the classroom routines the students are more apt to feel they belong.

Provides Structured Opportunities for Socialization

Some students do not get along with each other very well. Routines can be established to enable students to do activities together, such as take names for lunches. These routines provide students who may not interact appropriately with an opportunity to engage in an activity where there is high probability they will interact appropriately. In addition, the students who have poor social skills can be afforded a relatively safe opportunity to share a responsibility with another student and receive recognition and attention from peers and the teacher.

Basic Strategy for Establishing Classroom Routines

Classroom routines are simply a specific set of classroom expectations. Consequently, use the same instructional procedures described in Chapter 1 for teaching classroom expectations. The five teaching steps for establishing a routine are the same as those shown earlier in Table 3 (substitute "Routine" for "Expected Behavior"). An illustration of how to establish a routine is shown in Table 4.

Note: More structure is usually needed for younger students, larger groups of students, and classes comprised of a large number of students with problem behaviors.

TABLE 4: Example of Establishing a Classroom Routine

ROUTINE: Lining up to exit the classroom to other activities (lunch, recess, assemblies, library, P.E., buses, etc).
STEP ONE: Explain
Use a discussion format to describe the reasons for lining up when students leave the room. Some of the reasons are to be orderly, punctual, quiet, focused, respectful, and to be able to hear any last minute directions. Invite the students to contribute. Discuss ways in which they line up, such as who goes first and where the line should form. At the end of the discussion ask questions on why students need to line up and where and how the line is to form.
STEP TWO: Specify Student Behaviors
Describe in order the specific behaviors you want the students to follow. Signal at the end of the lesson that it is time for P.E. The students are expected to: 1. Put their materials away, clear their desks, and push in their chairs.   2. Move quietly, without rushing, to the doorway (in designated rows or when they have put their materials away).   3. Line up facing the door and keeping one space between each person.   4. Keep hands and feet to self.   5. Listen to the teacher and wait for the signal to depart. *(continued)*

STEP THREE: Practice

1. Ask the students to specify the behaviors in the routine for lining up.
2. Model the lining up routine.
3. Call on two or three students to model the routine and ask the rest of the class to watch carefully.
4. Call on other small groups to model the routine.
5. Call on the whole class to model the routine.
6. Repeat until all students demonstrate the routine correctly.
7. Acknowledge the students who cooperate with the practice session and follow the session with a brief reinforcing activity (to acknowledge cooperation).

STEP FOUR: Monitor

Give the signal to line up for P.E.
Directly observe the students. Praise students who complete the routine correctly and independently. Provide reminders or prompts to students who stall or engage in other behaviors. Provide specific praise and feedback on how the students performed once they have lined up at the door. For example, "Great, Michael and Louisa have left a space between them," or "José, Hayley, and Charlie, remember to face the door please." Monitor daily until no prompts are needed to complete the routine, after which monitor two or three times a week and then periodically.

STEP FIVE: Review

Conduct a brief discussion two or three weeks after the routine has been established. If there have been problems with the routine, conduct a practice session, monitor the routine more closely, and provide more frequent feedback. Do not take the routine for granted. Students need periodic reminders, corrections, and feedback to maintain a high standard of performance. Occasionally, provide a reward for good performance over time. For example, say, "I am really pleased with the way this class has been lining up over the past few weeks. You are being very responsible. I'd like to show my appreciation by giving you ten minutes of breaktime."

Common Classroom Routines

The following routines represent practices that are quite common in elementary classrooms. Teachers develop their own list of classroom routines with appropriate levels of detail to suit their purposes and needs. The following description of common classroom routines includes specific student behaviors and some suggestions. Teachers may adopt these practices or adapt the routines to meet their needs.

Starting the Day

Allow a set time, perhaps five minutes, to complete this routine. Teach this procedure during the first week of class. Be consistent in implementing the routine and review periodically.

STUDENT BEHAVIORS
• Put hats, coats, bags, and lunch boxes in designated areas. • Turn in homework or products to appropriate places. • Put instructional materials in desks. • Sharpen pencils and gather necessary materials for class. • Be seated and ready to start class by the time five minutes is up.

Entering the Classroom

This routine is very important since it will dictate how the class may proceed. If the students enter in an orderly manner, class may begin relatively quickly and efficiently. However, if students enter exhibiting noisy and excessive physical behavior, you will more than likely take considerable time to settle the children down and begin instruction. The entry routine is designed to ease the transition from activities outside the classroom to inside the classroom. Meet the students at the door or at least position yourself to monitor the students entering the classroom. Allow time to teach this routine and pay particular attention to explaining the importance of conversational voice instead of loud talk, walking versus rushing, keeping hands and feet to self, and moving directly to desks. Monitor and review this routine throughout the school year and carefully monitor difficult transitions such as coming in from recess or from an exciting assembly.

STUDENT BEHAVIORS

- Wait, line up at the door, or enter the room quietly.
- Use a conversational or "inside voice."
- Keep hands and feet to oneself.
- Walk.
- Move directly to desk or assigned area.
- Sit quietly and be ready for class.

Working Independently

Students are often required to work independently in activities such as reading, working on assignments or projects, or engaging in seatwork. The behavioral expectations are designed to assist the students to work independently. Establish activities for students who complete their work or assignment. Ensure these activities are of interest to the students so that they are reinforced for staying on task and finishing their work. Carefully establish a "quiet" room atmosphere to minimize distractions. Speak quietly and privately when assisting students, and avoid giving directions across the room. Have alternative work stations for the students to do their assignments. Some students may work better by themselves or in pairs, while others may prefer to work at a table beside other students. Make these options available and monitor which options best serve the students.

STUDENT BEHAVIORS

- Select area to work (usually at student's desk or a table).
- Have necessary materials ready.
- Work without talking.
- Raise hand or use signal to ask for assistance.
- Keep working or wait quietly for assistance when the teacher is helping someone else.
- Move quietly around the room when necessary.
- Put materials away when finished.
- Begin next activity when finished.

Using the Drinking Fountain

The most important part of this routine is to establish when the students may use the water fountain. Essentially, the fountain should be used during transition times or independent work times (coming in from recess, moving from in-class instruction to another activity). The fountain should not be used when instruction is underway.

STUDENT BEHAVIORS

- Use the fountain at the appropriate times (during transitions or independent work) and not during instruction.
- Use the fountain only for drinking (not for playing).
- Only one person is to be waiting to use the fountain.
- The person waiting should allow a little space.
- Put your mouth close to the fountain but not on the fountain.

Using the Restrooms

The main purpose of this routine is to have some control over the number of students out at a time and to know which students are out. In this way you will have more control over safety concerns as well as basic orderliness and cleanliness. Place emphasis on using the restrooms at regular times when all students are out of class, such as before school, at recess, at lunch time, or at passing time. Using the restroom during instruction should be the exception. However, when this does occur, use a wooden or plastic tag that is mounted in a visible place in the classroom. The students take the tag to the restroom and return it. In this way you and the students know if someone is at the restroom. If the restroom is in the classroom, leave the door ajar when it is not in use and closed when in use. Inspect the classroom restroom frequently to check for proper use and cleanliness. Provide instruction on proper use of the restroom, especially with younger students.

STUDENT BEHAVIORS

- Follow procedures for obtaining permission to use the restroom.
- Take the restroom tag with you.
- Use proper hygiene in the restroom (washing hands, drying hands).
- Put used paper towels in trash container.
- Return to class promptly.
- Return the tag to its proper place.
- Report any problems to your teacher (malfunctioning sinks, toilets, damage, excessive mess).

Sending Work Home

When work is sent home parents have an opportunity to see their children's products and assess their progress. The routine also serves as an opportunity for you and the parent(s) to communicate. One strategy is to use a large envelope with information printed on it such as date, comments, and a place for parent signature. A sample cover is presented in Figure 2.

FIGURE 2: Student Work Packet

Student Work Packet

Student Name _____		
Grade _____ Teacher _____		
Date	Comments	Parent Signature

Use this envelope on a regular basis (each week, term, or year). If the parent(s) have concerns or wish to discuss some aspect of the packet, respond quickly. Put great stress on the need for students to return the packet the next day. Strongly acknowledge students who cooperate, but allow some grace period for ones who may have forgotten. Provide strong reminders to students who do not return their packets. Solicit parent help in establishing this routine, but be aware that some parents may not cooperate. In this event contact the parent directly, explain the importance of the routine, and encourage him or her to return the packet. Use every opportunity—such as parent meetings and conferences, open house, and newsletters—to help the parents understand this process.

STUDENT BEHAVIORS

- Collect the work packet to take home.
- Deliver the packet to parent(s).
- Remind parent(s) to sign the packet and make comments.
- Return the packet to your teacher the next day.

Securing Assistance

Students need assistance on a fairly regular basis. A routine for securing assistance is necessary to ensure they get help in a timely manner. A common practice is to have the students raise their hand if they need help. (Note: They should raise the hand that is not used for writing so they may continue working.) This is fine if you can get to them reasonably quickly, but some students cannot continue working when they have one hand raised. Another practice is to have some kind of signal on each desk such as a sign. The student flips the sign to "help" when he or she needs assistance. If the students are working in a group, they can be required to ask other students in the group before they call on the teacher.

Some students may get into a pattern of asking for help too often. In these cases encourage them to try a little longer by themselves first and delay responding to them. Other students may develop a pattern of asking for help at the first sign of any difficulty. Urge them to try for two minutes before they ask for help. Again, practice the routine and review periodically.

STUDENT BEHAVIORS

- Always try by yourself first.
- Use the classroom signal for getting assistance.
- Keep working if you can or wait quietly.
- Remember the teacher has other students in the class that need help.

Moving Around the Classroom

Students may need to move around the classroom for supplies and other needs. However, if a routine is not established this movement can become disruptive. Establish when students may move in the room and when they should not move. Typically they remain in their seats during instruction and may move during transitions, independent work time, or small group work time. There should be an acceptable reason for the movement such as sharpening pencils, getting materials, using the water fountain, or returning books and materials. They should not move just to visit unless it is free time.

STUDENT BEHAVIORS

- Move in the classroom at the designated times (transitions, independent work, small group) and not during instruction.
- Move quietly and do not disturb others.
- Move directly to what you need and try not to waste time.

Establishing Class Helpers

Class helpers can provide you with assistance in managing some classroom responsibilities such as attendance, lunch orders, calendar announcements, distribution of bulletins and notices, and distribution of assignment sheets. The most important features of these routines are to carefully list the tasks to be completed, describe and model how the tasks are to be conducted, and develop a rotation system so that all students have the opportunity to participate.

> **STUDENT BEHAVIORS**
> - Take a turn.
> - Follow the procedures for completing the task.
> - Complete the task.

Speaking in Class

There will be many occasions when students will want to speak. Establish a routine to ensure that students have the opportunity to speak without disrupting the class. Many teachers require students to raise their hand and wait to be called on by the teacher or group leader. With smaller groups of students it may be possible for them to wait until someone else has finished speaking before they speak. Other routines can also be used such as unison responding, telling a partner, writing responses, or touching the answer in the book or materials. Model the routine and be very careful not to interrupt students, especially if they are expected to not interrupt others.

> **STUDENT BEHAVIORS**
> - Follow the procedure for speaking in class (raise your hand or wait your turn).
> - Be careful not to interrupt other students.
> - Try not to speak too loudly or too long.

Organizing Assignments

Students generate many products, assignments, and projects during the course of a year. In many cases the teacher grades or reviews the work and returns it to the students. It is very helpful to have a clear routine for managing these products. Dedicate an area in the room for students to place assignments to be turned in and another area for assignments that have been reviewed by the teacher. Bins could be used for these purposes. Review assignments and return them as quickly as possible. Provide time for students to make corrections on their work as needed. Provide the students with a place or file to put their work when they have completed the corrections or are finished with the assignment.

STUDENT BEHAVIORS

- Turn work into designated place.
- Collect work from the appropriate place.
- Make corrections as needed.
- Place corrected work in designated area or file.

Conducting Tests and Quizzes

Student assessment is a very common part of instruction. Establish a routine for taking tests and quizzes to ensure that student performance on the tests is a reliable measure of their ability. For example, if there is too much noise and movement, some students may not be able to concentrate or hear the questions. If there is talking, they may be helping each other. It is very important to practice the routine for test taking so that students are fluent with the procedures. One strategy is to conduct a practice test, without regard for the results of the test, so that students may become more familiar with the routine under more relaxed conditions.

STUDENT BEHAVIORS

- Put all materials away in your desk that are not needed for the test.
- Listen carefully to the teacher's directions (no talking).
- Raise your hand if you have a question or concern.
- Stay in your seat.
- Complete the test without talking or moving.
- Follow the procedure when you have finished the test (such as pass papers forward or give them to the class helper).
- Begin the activity following the test.

Meeting Personal Needs

Sometimes students may have personal needs such as sickness, a fear, or a problem that requires teacher support and resolution. Students need to have a way of connecting with the teacher for these situations. The basic issue is to have a routine that will enable the student to present the need with some level of privacy or confidentiality. The most critical feature is to provide the students with a signal to let you know there is a concern. The student may say, "I have a problem," or "I need your help with something personal." Keep in mind that the student may not be very articulate at this point. Usually the student's body language and verbal delivery will inform you that there is a problem. You may then afford the student privacy by taking him or her aside or visiting with the student at an opportune time away from other students. Carefully explain to the students that there are occasions when people need to be treated as individuals. On these occasions students need to know they can approach you and obtain assistance privately. Everyone else is expected to "mind their own business."

STUDENT BEHAVIORS

- Follow the class signal for letting the teacher know you have a private concern such as "Something is bothering me."
- Let the teacher know if you need help immediately or you can wait a while.
- Try to speak to the teacher privately and quietly if you do not want other students involved.

Using Filler Activities

Situations arise where a teacher has to be pulled away from instruction for a short time. For example, a student may have been hurt or a serious incident has occurred. In these cases you may be out of the room while another teacher keeps an eye on the class. There is not enough time for you to develop activities for the class as these situations arise. Develop some "sponge" activities that the students can be readily directed to undertake (such as reading, writing, individual projects, or finishing an assignment). Practice this routine from time to time. Remind the students they have been asked to be responsible while you are out for a few minutes, and expect that they can be successful. Provide feedback to the students on their performance when they are called on to engage in these activities. Strongly acknowledge students who cooperate, and provide reminders or negative consequences for noncooperative behavior.

STUDENT BEHAVIORS
• On the signal from the teacher, begin one of the selected activities.

Using Routines to Solve Problems

Establishing the routines described in this chapter will help prevent problem behavior. But routines can also be used for solving classroom problems. In the following example the class was having problems coming in from recess. A routine was established to address the problem.

Problem Scenario

When the students come back from recess, they rush to the classroom door talking loudly and pushing each other. There have been incidents of students hitting each other. The teacher finds it takes several minutes to settle the students down before the first activity can begin.

Possible Solution

Implement a routine for coming in from recess.

Schedule the necessary time to establish a routine for coming in from recess using the five steps described earlier for teaching a routine. An example of procedures for teaching this specific routine is presented in Table 5.

TABLE 5: Example of Establishing a Classroom Routine

ROUTINE: Coming in from recess.
STEP ONE: Explain
Secure the class' attention and describe the problem in coming in from recess. Explain that people are too noisy, there is too much pushing, and that students take a long time to settle down for class.
STEP TWO: Specify Student Behaviors
The class lines up at the door (the teacher meets the class at the door). Keep a space between each other. Use an "inside voice" (explain this concept). Wait for the signal to come into the classroom. Walk quietly and directly to your seat. Begin the assignment that is on the overhead (a math puzzle).
STEP THREE: Practice
Ask the class to describe the routine. Model the entry routine (teacher). A few students model the entry routine while everyone else watches. The class briefly discusses how these students performed (what was correct and what was incorrect, if anything). The whole class practices the routine.
STEP FOUR: Monitor
Remind the class of the routine just before recess. Be highly visible at the door when recess is over. Prompt the students on the routine where necessary. Provide feedback to the class on their performance. If performance is not satisfactory, schedule more practice. Strongly acknowledge good performance and provide some class-wide reinforcing activity.
STEP FIVE: Review
Provide periodic reviews of the students' performance; otherwise they may slip back into the previous problem behaviors. Use reminders intermittently.

Summary

Providing classroom instruction has become a very complex task for teachers. One strategy for reducing this complexity is to establish classroom routines. Essentially, identify a set of functional classroom routines and then provide systematic instruction to teach these routines. In this way a more cooperative and orderly classroom can be established.

chapter 3

Using Groups for
Instruction

IN A TYPICAL school day teachers have their students work individually, as a whole class, or in small groups within the class. A group is defined as two to ten students working together on some instructional activity. This chapter focuses on the various factors and procedures for maximizing the effectiveness of using groups during instruction. The following aspects of group work are presented: (1) Purpose and benefits; (2) Guidelines for group instruction; (3) Procedures for group instruction; and (4) Examples of group instruction.

Purpose and Benefits of Using Group Instruction

Matching the Students' Pace

When students are placed in a group based on their ability, there is a better chance that the activity will proceed at a rate commensurate with their ability. By contrast, if only whole class instruction is used, there is more likelihood that the slower students may be left behind and the quicker students may not be challenged.

Teacher Effectiveness

Typically, teachers find it easier to maintain attention, keep the students together, manage behavior, and provide instruction to groups of students compared to whole class instruction. Usually, the larger the class, the more difficult it is for the teacher to provide effective instruction.

Students Have More Opportunities to Take a Turn

Group instructional activities provide students with more opportunities to participate in the lesson, compared with large group activities. Essentially, each student has more opportunities to make responses or take a turn in small group instruction simply because there are fewer students competing for the available time.

Students Learn From Each Other

One of the major advantages of using small groups for instruction is that students have a better chance to learn from each other. With smaller groups it is easier for many students to attend to each other. For example, in large group or whole class instruction it is often difficult for a student to hear or see responses from other students. Small groups can be arranged so that students have an opportunity to attend to each other.

Assistance to Reticent Students

Some students, by their very nature or personality, find it difficult to make responses in front of the whole class. However, these students may find it easier to respond in a small group simply because the context is less public and less intimidating.

Social Skills Development

Most students need ongoing teaching and training in social skills. Group work provides a very natural context for providing students with an opportunity to work cooperatively, listen, show interest in and learn from each other, problem solve, manage disagreements, and take turns. In effect, the cooperative function of the group instruction sets the stage for opportunities to practice many social skills.

Opportunities for Student Leadership

There are several leaders within any class. When group instructional activities are used, more students receive opportunities to exercise leadership than would be possible in whole class instruction.

Guidelines for Group Instruction

Basic Approach

While group work is a very useful tool for instruction, it should not be the only form for instruction. Provide students with an opportunity to work in groups, whole class, and independent activities. The issue is not so much which form is better, but how to maximize each of these instructional methods. In other words, the schedule should be designed to accommodate a balance of whole class instruction, group work, and independent work.

Heterogenous Versus Homogenous Groups

There has been considerable debate and research on the issue of whether it is more effective to divide groups according to homogeneous groups (a grouping based on similar student characteristics such as skill levels or age) or heterogeneous groups (a randomized grouping such as mixed ability groupings). It is not the purpose of this book to discuss this issue in detail; however, Gamoran (1992) notes:

> "To place the debate in its proper perspective, we must remember that decisions about grouping are preliminary and that what matters most comes next: decisions about what to do with the students after they have been assigned to classes" (p.11).

Given that there are pros and cons for using groups, the following guidelines are designed to help teachers in the design and selection of groups for instruction:

1. Choose homogeneous groupings for curricula that have a linear progression in the development of skills and knowledge such as reading, writing, mathematics, and spelling. In these subjects the skills are arranged sequentially or linearly. Use heterogeneous groupings for curricula that have a nonlinear and holistic design such as art, physical education, and social studies projects.

2. Vary groups within the classroom and avoid permanent groupings across all subjects. For example, group the students according to ability during the math period and use different ability groupings for reading. Or, use homogenous groupings for math and heterogenous groupings for a social studies project.

3. Use heterogenous groupings to enhance social skills and self-esteem. When there is a mix of students within groups it is more likely that equity will be established.

4. Monitor student performance to ensure reasonable levels of achievement are occurring with all students and that all students are making appropriate progress. Otherwise, mediocrity in expectations and results will occur.

5. Provide more detailed instruction for the lower level students when homogenous groupings are used in basic skills. Generally, it is not satisfactory to use the same curriculum and same teaching strategies for all groupings. Students in the lower level groups often need a very carefully designed and structured curriculum for academic skills. In addition, these students need more assistance, a sharper focus on specific skills, more practice, and more review than their quicker counterparts.

Overall, use a planned mix of homogenous and heterogenous groupings within the classroom. With careful monitoring of student performance you will receive feedback on the best combinations of groupings to use.

Establishing Group Rules and Expectations

Be clear on how you want the group to function. Develop and teach rules and expectations. Common expectations for group work are:

- Taking a turn
- Waiting for someone to finish before you speak
- Listening to each other
- Using a "conversational" or "inside" voice
- Staying within your group and not joining in with adjacent groups
- Respecting others' opinions
- Avoiding negative comments
- Including all members in your group

Watch for Particular Problems

While there are many advantages to using groups for instruction, there are also some pitfalls that need to be anticipated and managed. Some of the common areas to watch are:

1. The dominant student. Sometimes one particular student will take over a group and limit or exclude the opportunities for other students to take a turn or participate. In this case, carefully explain the rules and expectations just before the students break out into their groups. Supervise the groups very closely and intervene or prompt the expected behaviors.

2. The nonparticipating student. Sometimes an individual will remain reticent, sit back, and not contribute to the group activity. Again, provide adequate supervision and prompt the student to join in the activity. Carefully stage activities if the student is very shy or withdrawn. If the student has limited skills, engineer parts of the activity so that he or she can offer partial responses that other students complete.

3. The dependent student. Some students may develop patterns where they never really learn independent responses. They participate in the group

in a partial manner. They wait for other students to start the activity and make very limited contributions. In effect, they may be participating, but they would not be able to begin and complete the task by themselves. Encourage and prompt these students to contribute more to the group. In addition, provide opportunities for independent activities so these students have the opportunity to function on their own and you can monitor their skill level.

Procedures for Small Group Instruction

Following are the steps for setting up group instruction. Each step is described, and examples will follow.

Steps for Group Instruction

STEP ONE
Forming the Groups

Use an assessment tool in the specific content area to form homogeneous or ability groups. Base placement within the groups on the student's performance. Decide on the number of groups that can be managed and divide the students accordingly. In general, divide the class into two or three groups.

In some cases it is desirable to form the groups between classes. For example, the third and fourth grade classes form a pool from which the groups are formed. There are several advantages to combining classes for group instruction: (1) The groups will be closer in ability levels; (2) Teachers may be able to teach to preferred ability levels; and (3) Students may receive more instructional time. The biggest problem with combining classes is that there is less flexibility with scheduling and a greater loss of time with students moving from class to class.

Use a randomized system to form heterogeneous groups (mixed ability groupings). For example, if the teacher decides to form three groups, students may be given the number one, two, or three. Divide the students according to the number selected.

STEP TWO
Developing a Schedule

Pay careful attention to developing a schedule for group instruction. It is particularly important to keep the schedule when the groups are formed between classes. Teacher relationships can become strained when one teacher does not have students ready for group instruction while the other teacher is waiting. Frustration can also occur when one teacher frequently wants to change the schedule. In general, pay careful attention to developing the schedule and be sure to follow it with a reasonable degree of urgency and consistency.

STEP THREE
Establishing Behavior Expectations

Student behavior, in a large measure, will determine whether the group instruction will be successful or not. Clearly establish a routine for group instruction and systematically teach the routine. A routine for group instruction usually involves three components: (1) Start-up behaviors (These behaviors include transitioning to the group, bringing the necessary materials, and moving to the designated area.); (2) Behavioral expectations during group instruction; and (3) An exit routine (putting materials away and transitioning to the next activity). Follow the procedures described in Chapter 2, Establishing Classroom Routines, for teaching the routines for group instruction.

STEP FOUR
Establishing Group Objectives

Establishing objectives is important for any form of instruction, including group instruction. It is particularly important to specify the objectives when the group largely directs itself, as in a group project. Clarifying the group objectives will help students stay focused. Otherwise, they may become off task or spend too much time on some of the components and not complete the project. It may be necessary to break the objectives into steps and establish timelines for each step so the project can be completed within the specified time frame. Keep in mind, while the process of involvement may be rewarding to students, they also need to experience bringing the activity to closure.

S T E P   F I V E
Teaching the Group Process

Do not assume that students know how to function productively in a group. Take time to explain and teach the steps of a group process. Use the instructional procedures described in Chapters 1 and 2 for teaching classroom expectations and routines. Engage the students in some activities that are specifically designed to teach the group process. Critical group process skills for students are to:

- Take turns appropriately.
- Listen to each others' responses.
- Encourage responses from all members of the group.
- Brainstorm ideas and prioritize responses.

Common strategies for teaching group behaviors are:

Roundtable—The group is assigned a question with many possible responses. Students make a list on one piece of paper with each student writing a response and passing on the list to the next person. In this way a group response is obtained with each group member contributing.

Roundrobin—This activity is the verbal counterpart to Roundtable. The students take turns verbally stating their responses to the assigned question.

Brainstorming—A time limit is set for the group to generate their list of responses. The group then prioritizes the responses by vote. Each member of the group is expected to vote.

Competition—Activities can be arranged involving competition between groups. Usually criteria are set such as the most examples or the first group to complete all the tasks within a set time. Competition should be used to create group spirit but should not be overused. Otherwise, the class may become divided or some groups may not try if they continually "lose."

STEP SIX
Monitoring Group Performance

Provide active supervision to ensure the groups are functioning appropriately. Make pauses when teaching one group to observe other students who may be engaged in independent work or some group activity. Acknowledge students who are on track and following expectations. Similarly, prompt and remind students who are not following the procedures. In this way appropriate behavior can be maintained, and problem behavior can be addressed immediately.

STEP SEVEN
Providing Group Feedback

At the close of group work, allow time to provide feedback to the students on their performance during group instruction. Direct the feedback toward:

- Positive examples of students following the behavioral expectations.
- Positive examples of group process behaviors.
- Concerns about problems and encouragement to do better next time.
- Specific concerns or areas addressed for the particular group work of the day.
- Group products or outcomes that merit specific attention.
- Delivering rewards or reinforcers for exemplary performance and consequences as necessary for problem behavior (see Chapter 5 for examples of rewards and consequences).

STEP EIGHT
Establishing Exit Routines

Provide the students with sufficient time to exit the group instruction activity and move toward the next activity on the schedule. Materials may need to be put away, chairs and tables rearranged, products turned in to the teacher or a designated area, and work areas cleaned. Each student should contribute to the exit procedures. Teach the exit routine in the classroom before group work is conducted. Attention to the exit routine will ensure that the students will approach the next activity in an orderly and focused manner.

STEP NINE
Amending Groups

Review and revise the groups on a regular basis. It is a judgment call as to how long a group should stay intact. If the time is too short the group processes may not develop. On the other hand, if the groups stay together too long, problems may arise, such as increases in off-task behavior and unnecessary interactions between groups. Monitor the groups carefully for student performance and on-task behavior. The monitoring information will dictate when to amend the groups.

Table 6 illustrates examples of group instruction.

TABLE 6: Examples of Group Instruction

Example 1: Teacher-Directed Group Instruction on Reading in an Individual Class
Ms. Jones is a third grade teacher with 28 students in her class. She uses the following procedures to form three groups to teach reading:
STEP ONE: Forming the Groups Ms. Jones collects the testing results from the previous year, Grade 2, located in the office. She also administers the Gray Oral Reading Test, since there are new students and some of her students may have regressed over the summer break. On the basis of these results she divides the class into three equal groups. The groups are called Group 1, Group 2, and Group 3.
STEP TWO: Developing a Schedule The reading block is scheduled daily for 55 minutes, 9:00 AM to 9:55 AM. The 55 minutes is divided into three time slots allowing three minutes for transition. Group 1   9:00 - 9:16 Group 2   9:19 -9:34 Group 3   9:37 - 9:52 Ms. Jones has specifically prepared seat work for the students who are not receiving instruction. She makes sure the students are underway with their seatwork within the three minute transition time before she starts reading instruction with one of the groups.
STEP THREE: Establishing Behavior Expectations Ms. Jones develops a set of behavior expectations for the students doing seatwork and for those receiving group instruction. The behaviors are practiced beforehand. Students doing seatwork are expected to work quietly by themselves, ask for help from a partner if necessary, move around the room quietly if necessary, and not interrupt the group instruction. Students receiving group instruction are expected to participate to the best of their abilities, take a turn, wait and listen when someone else is taking a turn, join in group responses, and conduct transitions quickly and quietly.
STEP FOUR: Establishing Group Objectives Ms. Jones explains to each group their present level of reading in the program. She clearly indicates what they will be working on during the lesson and what they are expected to learn.   (continued)

STEP FIVE: Teaching the Group Process

Ms. Jones has already conducted practice sessions on student behavior in group instruction. She has emphasized how the behaviors will help the students become better readers. She also provides regular reminders to the groups on these behaviors.

STEP SIX: Monitoring Group Performance

Ms. Jones monitors the students' performance on the reading tasks and activities during the group instruction. In addition, she periodically scans the students doing seatwork and acknowledges their behavior.

STEP SEVEN: Providing Group Feedback

At the end of the lesson Ms. Jones informs the students of their progress during the lesson, providing specific feedback as necessary. She also provides feedback to the students doing seatwork.

STEP EIGHT: Establishing Exit Routines

On the signal that the group instruction is finished, the students move quickly and quietly to the next activity. The students are expected to complete the transition steps independently. Ms. Jones has addressed and practiced the transition routine with the class before group instruction occurs. She also provides periodic reminders, practice, and feedback to the students on the transition routines. Ms. Jones works hard to have the transition completed within the set three minutes.

STEP NINE: Amending Groups

The groups are adjusted at the end of the first month. The groupings are usually amended based on student progress. The groups are amended several times throughout the year.

Example 2: Teacher-Directed Group Instruction With Combined Classes for Math

Ms. Jones is a member of the third grade team with three other teachers. Ms. Jones and the team use the following procedures to group the students for math.

STEP ONE: Forming the Groups

The four teachers meet to review assessment information and form the groups for math. Testing information is obtained from: (1) Test scores from the previous year; (2) Input from teachers from the previous year, if possible; and (3) Results of test scores administered by the present teachers. On the basis of this assessment information the four teachers divide the pool of students into four homogeneous groups and decide among themselves which group they prefer to teach.

STEP TWO: Developing a Schedule

A block of time is dedicated to math instruction across the four classes. For example, math is scheduled for 45 minutes from 10:00 AM to 10:45 AM. Each teacher makes a commitment to keep this schedule; otherwise, the system will erode if any teacher is consistently late. Each teacher pays particular attention to the start time and end time. Students must be ready to move at 10:00 AM and be in their own classroom by 10:45 AM.

STEP THREE: Establishing Behavior Expectations

Teachers reach agreement on expected behavior within each group and manage the groups in a uniform manner. Consistency in management of the groups makes it easier for students who may have to move when the groups are amended (Step Nine). The behavioral expectations also include transition routines to ensure that students bring the needed materials for class. Students should not have to return to their classroom for supplies.

STEP FOUR: Establishing Group Objectives

Group objectives for math will be built into the curriculum. These objectives are made clear to the students. In addition, objectives regarding behavior are also specified.

STEP FIVE: Teaching the Group Process

Each teacher systematically teaches the expected behaviors for group work and the transition to and from the respective group sites. The four teachers periodically discuss student behavior at their regular meetings (see Step Ten).

STEP SIX: Monitoring Group Performance

Each teacher carefully monitors student performance on progress in math, on behavior in group instruction, and in following the transition routines. Results are discussed at the regular meetings between the four teachers. (continued)

STEP SEVEN: Providing Group Feedback

Just before the end of each group session the teachers provide feedback to their group. Results obtained from Step Six, "Monitoring," provide the basis for this feedback on learning progress, behavior in the group, and following the transition routine.

STEP EIGHT: Establishing Exit Routines

The four teachers develop an exit routine. This routine is taught to each class. Teachers review the adequacy of the exit routine on a regular basis at their meetings.

STEP NINE: Amending Groups

The groups are amended on a periodic basis throughout the year based on student performance. Typically, groups are amended midterm and at the end of the term.

STEP TEN: Conduct Regular Teacher Meetings

The four teachers meet on a regular basis to discuss how the groups are working, problems that may arise and respective solutions, amendments to groups, curricular issues, and other specific concerns. These meetings are held on a weekly basis. The teachers hold short frequent meetings rather than long infrequent meetings. The meetings start and end punctually, and one teacher keeps records for these meetings (this task is rotated between the four teachers).

Example 3: Student-Directed Group Project

The second grade teacher plans to center a class activity on "The Oregon Trail." The students were informed of the activity.

STEP ONE: Forming the Groups

A list of ten topics related to "The Oregon Trail" such as materials for the trip, supplies, route, maps, climate or weather to be prepared for is generated by the class. Post the list and ask students to choose a topic. Stipulate that no more than three students can sign up for one topic. Draw the students' names out of a box; each student then signs up for a topic until all slots are filled.

STEP TWO: Developing a Schedule

Identify a closing date, perhaps four weeks from the start date or a date that coincides with a special date such as an open house day. Schedule a daily block of time for the students to work together on the project. Students may also work on their project during their free time. Be prepared to allocate more time as the closing date approaches, especially if the product is to be used for a public display at a set time.

STEP THREE: Establishing Behavior Expectations

Since this project is essentially student directed, carefully teach the expected behaviors. Stress the need to work cooperatively, share materials, allow all students to contribute, use materials properly, and have overall pride in the work. In addition, establish clear expectations for students to stay within their own group and to avoid becoming engaged with other groups.

STEP FOUR: Establishing Group Objectives

Make it very clear to the students that a product is required, and display projects from other years as examples. In addition, options such as charts, models, visual examples, media examples, pictures, and drawings are identified and described. Since a presentation is required, specify the length of time required and the need to have roles for all members of the group.

STEP FIVE: Teaching the Group Process

Carefully explain the specific steps and timelines for the project. The steps include content, research, visual forms, narrative, and presentation.

STEP SIX: Monitoring Group Performance

Stations are designated for each group with adequate spaces between each group. Supervise actively while the students are engaged in the group activity. Move around, interact briefly, and provide prompts as necessary to keep the students on track and all students involved. Provide students additional assistance as needed for problem solving and working together appropriately. Allocate an area for students to store their unfinished and finished products.

STEP SEVEN: Providing Group Feedback

Just before the end of each group session, particularly in the early sessions, inform the students of their progress with their projects and their cooperation with the behavior expectations. Praise and acknowledge the students for following the expectations. Provide encouragement and reminders for the students who do not follow the expectations. (continued)

STEP EIGHT: Establishing Exit Routines

As in the previous two examples, establish an exit routine so that students will finish their work punctually with materials and products put away and stations cleaned as necessary. Give signals ahead of time such as, "We have five minutes left to get everything put away." Appoint a student monitor in each group to ensure that the exit routine is followed.

STEP NINE: Amending Groups

Groups are not usually amended for this kind of group work. Some students may need to be moved to another group on the basis of problem behavior or personal conflicts, but these cases should be exceptions.

Summary

Group work is an instructional tool that can assist the learning process. Use the tool in conjunction with other classroom activities to balance teaching procedures for whole class activities, group work, and independent work. Give careful attention to selecting the groups and instructional activities designed for the groups. There are pros and cons for heterogenous and homogenous groups. Develop a balance between the groups and continually monitor student performance to ensure they are developing the targeted skills at a reasonable rate. To weigh the advantages of the three types of grouping—whole class, small group, and individual—ask the summary questions presented in the following table.

QUESTIONS FOR ADDRESSING GROUPING ARRANGEMENTS
Whole Class
· What are the students learning from each other?
· Are students disrupting the class as a whole?
· How engaged is the class as a whole?
Small Group
· On what basis should students be grouped? And with whom?
· What are other students doing during group instruction?
· How long should groups be conducted? And where?
Individual
· Who can teach the student individually? And where?
· How do skills and responses transfer and generalize to other nonindividualized settings?

(Adapted with permission from Sugai & Tindal, 1993, p. 308)

chapter 4

> Managing
> Instruction

ONE OF THE most disturbing trends facing educators today is that less time is spent on actual instruction in the classroom. Researchers have reported the following findings:

- Teachers spend anywhere from 40 to 75% of available instructional time in activities other than instruction.

- Students spend as little as 17% of their classroom time successfully engaged in academic tasks.

- A typical intermediate grade level averaged 38 minutes of instruction out of a three-hour period. (Walker, Colvin, & Ramsey, 1995)

While there are many pressures facing educators today such as the need to increase the quality of education, raise achievement test scores, and effectively manage an increasingly diverse student population—all with diminishing funds—there are strategies that teachers can use to increase the amount of time in which teaching and learning can occur. The purpose of this chapter is to present strategies for maximizing instructional time and increasing learning in the classroom. There is considerable variability in teaching procedures, curriculum choices, and assessment requirements from district to district and from state to state, so the following information is presented more as general guidelines than specific procedures. Individual teachers will need to carefully examine the directions and requirements of their district in order to plan the necessary details for delivering instruction. Four areas are addressed: (1) Student assessment; (2) Curriculum planning; (3) General strategies for delivering instruction; and (4) Intervening during instruction.

Student Assessment

Typically, teachers engage in three levels of student assessment: (1) Initial placement; (2) Progress measures; and (3) Mastery.

Initial Placement—These tests are designed to assess the current level of functioning of the students. The purpose is to place students either in groups, classes, or programs. For example, if the teacher uses ability groupings for reading (see Chapter 3: Using Groups for Instruction), a reading test is administered, and students with comparable scores are placed in the same groups. Similarly, a placement procedure is used to see if students have the necessary preskills for a topic or whether they should be placed at an advanced point in the program. Or, if a specific curriculum program is used, for example, *Reading Mastery* (Engelmann & Bruner, 1983), a placement test is conducted to determine where the students start in the program.

Table 7 illustrates an example of student groupings based on a math placement test that is comprised of 55 questions sampling the range of content covered during grades 3-6. The students are placed in ability groups based on their scores. For example, any students in grades 3-6 who score in the range of 20-25 are placed in Group One (i.e., they are performing at a grade 3 level. Students who score in the range of 50 or more would be placed in Group Four (i.e., they are performing at a grade 6 level of ability).

The Effective Elementary Classroom

TABLE 7

STUDENT GROUPINGS BASED ON MATH PLACEMENT TEST		
Group	Grade Level	Score on Placement Test
One	3rd	20-25
Two	4th	26-39
Three	5th	40-49
Four	6th	50+

Note: Keep in mind that errors can occur with placement testing. It may be possible that a student has the main skills to be taught, but performs poorly on the particular test. The judgments made on placement tests should be tentative and subject to revisions based on subsequent student performance.

Progress Measures—These topic-area tests are designed to monitor student progress during instruction. Information is obtained to determine: (1) If students are learning the targeted skills; (2) To identify error patterns so that timely corrections can be made; and (3) To obtain feedback on the appropriateness of the curriculum or the curriculum placement. These measures are largely informal such as a question-answer format or short written responses. To ensure that the questions provide reliable and valid information, the strategies listed in Table 8 are recommended.

TABLE 8

STRATEGIES TO ENSURE HIGH QUALITY RESPONSES TO QUESTIONS
1. Keep all students on task.
2. Phrase questions clearly.
3. Provide a wait time (typically three to five seconds).
4. Respond to students' answers positively and constructively.
5. Ask questions frequently. *(continued)*

6. Ask students questions in all phases (before, during, and after) of instruction.

7. Focus questions on academic content.

8. Focus questions on a variety of knowledge forms and in response to different text structures.

9. Consider a variety of learning tasks and student responses needed to answer the questions.

10. Be systematic and consistent in question-asking with controlled practice provided for strategies in answering the questions.

11. Ask questions that result in a high rate of success.

12. Encourage students to respond in some fashion, whether they are certain of the answer or not.

13. If students are incorrect, provide assistance or the correct answer along with an explanation.

14. Balance selection of respondents between students who volunteer and those who don't.

(Reprinted with permission from Sugai & Tindal, 1993, p. 330)

Progress measures during instruction can also be determined by establishing predetermined criteria for the rate at which units are completed to ensure that all curriculum content is covered during the year. For example, if a school district requires three units of science to be taught in grade 4, the teacher needs to develop a weekly schedule to ensure the units are taught. A unit may be defined as completion of a certain number of pages in the workbook, by a specified number of exercises in the text, by performance on a test on key concepts, or by the amount of work to be covered in a day or a week. These units provide the teacher with a measure for determining progress through a curriculum.

Mastery Assessment—These tests are designed to determine if students have achieved the competencies or skills addressed in the instructional program. The tests are typically administered at the end of large blocks of instructional time such as at the end of a six-week period, the end of the term, and the end of the year. The tests can be teacher-made or standardized tests with high reliability and validity.

Informal or teacher-made tests are designed to assess whether the students can demonstrate, independently, mastery of a new skill. These tests serve the teacher directly and usually do not have reliability and validity measures. Four general guidelines are recommended for developing these tests in Table 9.

TABLE 9

GUIDELINES FOR DEVELOPING INFORMAL MASTERY TESTS

1. Use untrained examples for test items.

2. Request demonstrations (permanent products) of the skill rather than oral answers.

3. If possible, test in the natural context (for example, the classroom or playground).

4. Withhold feedback until the complete skill has been demonstrated.

Formal tests for mastery have the properties of reliability and validity and serve much broader purposes. These tests, typically called achievement tests (such as the Metropolitan Achievement Test, Comprehensive Test of Basic Skills, and the Test of Cognitive Skills), are designed to compare the results with other groups of students. The results may be rank ordered across schools within the state or the nation. Or more simply, the results may indicate whether these students are performing at grade level or not. Formal achievement tests have standardized procedures for administration and scoring. These tests are typically scheduled by the school district. While the tests may be very broad and not sensitive to individual curricula, the comparative information can be helpful in providing broad-based comparisons of student performance on academic skills.

Curriculum Planning

In this step the teacher plans the content of what will be taught throughout the school year. Again, there is large variability in how much latitude a teacher has in making decisions regarding curriculum and content areas in U. S. public schools. Consequently, individual teachers will need to be guided by their local and state authorities. The following general guidelines are recommended in planning the curricula for the year:

Develop time lines for the specific content to be covered during the year. Divide the year into blocks of 6-8 weeks and assign units or modules of content to each block. Ensure that the content assigned during the first week of school is relatively straightforward so the students can be engaged readily and you can address the many start-up tasks.

Identify materials for each unit and make sure the necessary materials, supplies, and textbooks are available before the unit begins.

List activities for each unit. Develop a chart listing content units, materials, and activities for each unit.

Identify testing procedures for content areas where precise information is needed for placement in programs or units and for assigning students to groups. Obtain test results from previous testing that may be available from student records. Develop, print, and organize tests you plan to administer yourself at the start of the year in case you have new students or previous records are insufficient.

Determine student groupings for content areas where you have decided to use ability groupings within your classroom or for team teaching. Plan to conduct appropriate testing in the first week of school if you do not have sufficient information to form the groups before school starts.

Delivering Instruction

In a well-designed classroom, careful attention is given to the use of effective teaching strategies. These strategies increase instructional time and student learning. In addition, a strong relationship exists between effective teaching practices and positive student behavior. If all students are actively engaged in the lesson at hand, the chances of problem behavior occurring are small. Some recommended effective strategies for delivering instruction are described as follows.

Instructional Objectives

Students are more likely to learn when given instructional objectives. Objectives enable measurement of acquisition, maintenance and generalization, and teaching to criterion, and they serve as a road map to show students what they are learning and the relevance of each lesson.

Examples of Instructional Objectives:

- By the end of the month you will be able to name all the states on a blank map of the U.S.

- By the end of the week you will be able to identify the verb(s) in a sentence.

- By the end of the year you will be writing in cursive style.

Teaching to Mastery

Mastery learning assumes that the vast majority of students can master specific skills if they are given sufficient time to learn the skill, along with appropriate help, feedback, and practice. Students with learning and behavior problems typically have an academic profile that reflects "splinter skills." That is, they have not reached mastery on component skills in subject areas such as math and reading. Consequently, as each new skill is introduced, these students have difficulty catching up or staying with the group. Becker (1986) identified several steps for establishing mastery learning:

Mastery Learning Steps

1. Specify objectives.
2. Assess pre-skills for appropriate placement.
3. Develop proactive and positive procedures for active learning.
4. Utilize best practice instructional procedures to teach objectives.
5. Allow individual students appropriate time to reach mastery.
6. Assess frequently and systematically.
7. Monitor student progress during initial learning.
8. Provide ongoing feedback.
9. Provide corrective and remedial strategies as needed.
10. Provide adequate practice to master subskills and component skills.

(Adapted from Becker, (1986).)

Rates of Success

All students need to experience an adequate rate of success; otherwise, they will become bored or frustrated and probably engage in problem behavior. Planning for student success requires teachers to carefully select appropriate materials and instructional activities, and to monitor student progress.

Pacing

Teachers sometimes wonder if their presentation is too fast or too slow. This teaching variable, called pacing, deals with the number of per-period chances students have to respond academically. Students are generally more attentive, more on task, and make fewer errors during high-rate presentations than during low-rate presentations. In general, it's better to be too fast than too slow. Fast-pacing encourages on-task behavior, while slow pacing may allow off-task and inappropriate behavior.

Planned Variation of Instruction

There are many strategies for delivering instruction such as teacher-directed, cooperative learning activities, independent work, small group work, lecture formats, and discussion activities. While some of these strategies may be more effective with some classes, the important overall strategy is to use planned variation. Students' attention will be lost if they are engaged in any one strategy for too long. Plan to change the delivery of instruction before the students' attention is lost. A brief description of delivery systems for instruction is presented in Table 10.

TABLE 10

DELIVERY SYSTEMS FOR INSTRUCTION

1. *Lectures.* The most dominant format for delivering instruction in which the teacher directs all verbal interactions typically in a monologue and separated from the listener by several feet.

2. *Recitation.* Repetition of stock material by a student or students, directed entirely by the teacher or the curriculum materials.

3. *Demonstrations.* Presentation of models by the teacher so the students can see what they are learning and what they will eventually be demonstrating.

4. *Discussion.* An exchange with students facilitated by the teacher on a specific topic; gives both teacher and students opportunities to respond to each other's contributions.

5. *Question/answer.* A student-directed delivery system that provides opportunities for individual input and presents loosely guided parameters about what to say.

6. *Oral practice.* Like recitation, provides a structured delivery system in which students must devise responses. (continued)

7. Film/TV/AV. A third-party delivery system in which the teacher is usually proctoring in the room.

8. Textbook/worksheet. Presentation of information as a permanent product, which students must interact with in order to access new or review information.

9. Games and contests. Presentation of "problems" in game or contest situation; students must use some rule or algorithm to solve the problem.

10. Project/computer. Use of computers to deliver instruction with either a drill/practice activity or a game format; teachers can also assign projects in which students engage in independent study.

(Reprinted with permission from Sugai & Tindal, 1993, p. 309.)

Teacher-Student Interactions

Interactions refer to responses between a teacher and student(s). They can either be initiated by the teacher or by the student. If most interactions are student initiated, the question arises, "Who is teaching whom?" or "Who's in charge here?" On the other hand, if nearly all the interactions are teacher initiated, it could mean the students are too passive or uncreative. Either extreme is unacceptable. In a structured classroom, an adequate balance between teacher- and student-initiated interactions is seven to three.

Teacher-student interactions can either be positive or negative, depending on whether a teacher is responding to acceptable or inappropriate behavior. A useful guideline is to expect at least 80 to 85% of all interactions to be positive.

On-Task Behavior

To achieve on-task behavior among students, secure and maintain their attention. This can be tricky. Teachers cannot assume that students will automatically be motivated to learn what is taught. Plan to carefully stage instruction to capture the students' interest and to involve them by actively engaging them in the lesson. A realistic expectation for having students on task (for example, paying attention to the teacher, participating in class discussion, or working independently) is at least 80% of their allocated instructional time.

Managing Student Errors

Correcting student errors is an important part of the instructional process. Error correction procedures need to be systematic, timely, and positive. A common procedure is to make the student aware of an error, provide additional information on how to correctly respond, and then test on the same example.

Pay particular attention to error rates. A high error rate can mean material is too difficult and the student may become frustrated. Conversely, a low error rate can mean the work is too easy and boredom may result. In either case, problems may arise that may divert the teacher and student from the instructional activities. A recommended balance is to design instruction so that corrections occur about 30% of the time and correct performance occurs 70% of the time. For example, frequently obtain performance measures from students through quizzes, assignments, and question/answer sessions. Student scores will dictate whether adjustments need to be made with the content.

Also, keep track of the kinds of errors students make. Analyzing errors, or error patterns, provides helpful information on teacher presentations, choice of examples, error correction procedures, and rules that may need revision.

Shaping Student Responses

Students need to be encouraged to respond to instruction during class. Careful use of teacher attention and approval (for example, "good job," "nice effort," "you're improving") can increase student productivity and participation. Use differential praise to shape responses (for example, "Excellent" for high criterion work and "Great, you're getting the hang of it" for work that is very close to criterion). Frequent use of such reinforcement is highly recommended for improving task completion, accuracy, and time to complete tasks.

Managing Student Assignments

Teachers typically provide students with assignments as a part of instruction. These assignments provide teachers with ongoing information on how the students are progressing. Once students turn in their work, it is important to have a reasonably quick turnaround. In this way the students get feedback they can put to immediate use. However, if there is a long delay, students may not put the feedback to use and may lose motivation for completing subsequent assignments. On the other hand, the teacher may spend an enormous amount of personal time if all assignments are individually graded. It is imperative to develop a plan that will enable a prompt return of work and at the same time minimize the amount of time a teacher has to spend grading.

One strategy for meeting these needs is to develop a plan that involves a combination of quizzes and written assignments. The quizzes provide information on skill knowledge, while the assignments can be used for skill practice. A key strategy is to involve the students in correcting the assignments and quizzes. Essentially, the teacher leads the correction, while the students correct and score each other's work. Sometimes students can correct their own work. In these cases they correct their work with colored pencils to highlight the corrections. Papers are returned with follow-up as needed.

Intervening During Instruction

Teachers can maintain quality instruction and prevent a number of problem behaviors by paying careful attention to the strategies just described for delivering instruction. However, students may become off task and problem behaviors may arise. This section examines strategies for intervening during instruction to maintain instruction and prevent further problem behavior.

Establish an Entry Activity

An independent activity helps to settle down students as they come into class (such as a math puzzle or copying outlines from the overhead). These activities provide a focus for the students, reduce student interactions, and provide an opportunity for the teacher to prompt a task. These entry activities are particularly important where the lesson at hand involves some set-up time such as in an art class.

Keep Initial Explanations Brief

Keep in mind that lengthy explanations at the beginning of a lesson set the stage for off-task and disruptive behavior. The quicker students are engaged in an on-task activity the less likelihood there will be problem behavior. If several pieces of information must be presented, they should be distributed over the period.

Secure Everyone's Attention Before Beginning Explanations

In general it is important to secure everyone's attention before beginning an explanation or lesson; otherwise, students may learn that they do not need to listen. To gain the students' attention, position yourself so you can see the faces of all your students and ensure that all of the students are looking at you. Some teachers use signals to gain students' attention. For example, make the statement, "Everyone listen," change volume, hold up a hand, scan the whole class, look toward nonlistening students to get their attention, and acknowledge students who are attending. Sometimes it may be appropriate to get the class moving into an activity, reinforce the cooperative students, and redirect the remaining students.

Plan for Difficult Transitions

Transitions are probably the most common setting for problem behavior. Problems will often arise if these transitions are not carefully planned. Transitions can be managed effectively by introducing intermediate steps, providing advance prompts and reminders, and reinforcing students who cooperate. Examine your programs frequently to identify difficult transitions and make appropriate adjustments. Many problems arise from poor planning when students are rushed at the end of one activity and have to scramble to the next one. If students begin to get out of control or depart significantly from a planned activity, introduce an independent activity to settle them down. For example, direct the students to write some responses. Once students have calmed down, resume the activity or move on to something else. Also, have a set signal for stopping an activity, such as an arm raised or a verbal cue.

Use Direct Speech

Language should be kept as simple, respectful, and direct as possible. Avoid using questions if your intent is to present a direction. Also, long and lengthy explanations in the context of correcting a student may cause additional problem behavior.

Avoid Dead Time

Students need to know what they should be doing at all times; otherwise, they may generate their own (inappropriate) activities. Essentially, students must not have "dead time." It is helpful to have back-up or "sponge" activities in case a lesson is completed before the end of a period. Have alternative activities ready for students who finish an activity while others need extra assistance. "Sponge" activities, as the name suggests, can be used to engage students during transition activities. These activities should be constructive and somewhat reinforcing, and the students involved should need minimal assistance with them. Examples of these activities include:

- Games
- Puzzles
- Drawing
- Coloring
- Reading a book of choice
- Various activity centers
- Choices of activities drawn from a box

Settle Students Down Near the End of Each Period

Develop a routine to settle students down before the end of a class period. In this way the students are likely to make a quicker and calmer transition to the next period. Also, teachers appreciate colleagues who send students along to other classes and activities in a calm (rather than rushed, agitated, or excited) manner.

Establish an exit routine of students with your colleagues. For example, after a special activity under the direction of another teacher, it should be clear whether you come to retrieve the class or whether the other teacher will supervise the returning students.

Summary

One of the major goals for all teachers is to provide effective instruction. However, if we are not careful, instructional time can be substantially eroded. The purpose of this chapter was to focus on key variables that help teachers maximize the time they dedicate to instruction. These variables included systematic assessment, curriculum planning, strategies for delivering instruction, and procedures for intervening on problem behavior during instruction. Effective control of these teaching tools will increase instructional time, maximize student learning, and minimize problem behavior.

Preventing Problem Behavior

EVEN THOUGH A teacher does an excellent job in organizing the classroom, affording adequate structure, and providing quality instruction, problem behavior may still arise. One reason is that there may be spillover effects from the home or community. For example, problems may arise as a result of poverty, community crime, lack of supervision, dysfunctional homes, substance abuse, diet, health factors, peer pressure, and gang activity. In addition, some students have problem behaviors that are very well established, and they may exhibit these behaviors periodically even in the best of classrooms. In order to limit the spillover effects of these problems, you need to establish a strong behavior management system in the classroom.

A basic rule for the relationship between behavior and learning is: Good behavior enables learning to take place, while problem behavior disrupts the teaching/learning process. The goal of the behavior management system is to establish good behavior and to minimize problem behavior. The next two chapters present information and procedures for developing systems for managing problem behavior. In this chapter, the focus is on systems to maintain acceptable behavior and prevent problem behavior. In the next chapter, systems for managing problem behavior after it has occurred are addressed.

The best approach to maintaining expected behavior and preventing problem behavior is to use proactive strategies to provide quality instruction and to teach expected behavior. The three basic approaches are: (1) Establishing classroom expectations; (2) Developing effective consequences; and (3) Utilizing effective instructional management techniques.

Establishing Classroom Expectations

Review the information presented in Chapter 1. The summary steps in developing and implementing classroom expectations are:

- Discuss and explain the behavioral expectations to the class.
- Provide opportunities to practice the expectations via behavioral expectations, modeling, simulations, role plays, and other appropriate activities.
- Post the expectations and refer to them frequently.
- Provide frequent reminders of the rules, prompts, and consistent feedback.
- Provide high rates of reinforcement for students who exhibit the expected behaviors and systematic correction procedures for students who do not cooperate.
- Review the expectations on a regular basis.

Developing Effective Consequences

The basic purpose in using consequences in a behavior management plan is to give a clear and consistent message to the students that good behavior leads to positive consequences, while problem behavior leads to negative consequences. In this way positive consequences serve to reinforce expected behavior and negative consequences serve to reduce or eliminate problem behavior.

Using Positive Consequences

Careful and consistent use of positive consequences for demonstrations of expected behavior is the surest strategy for establishing and maintaining expected behavior. The main rules for using positive consequences are:

1. Deliver the consequences frequently (especially for younger children and for children who have problem behavior).

2. Deliver the consequences consistently and as immediately as possible.

3. Emphasize social reinforcers versus tangible reinforcers as much as possible.

4. Have some delayed and longer-term reinforcers.

5. Vary reinforcers.

6. Maintain a consistent criteria for reinforcers.

Examples of positive consequences for good behavior are:

- Teacher praise and demonstrations of teacher approval (e.g., "I appreciate the quiet way the class is working.")
- Points earned by individual students, groups of students, or the whole class for certain rewards or privileges
- Privileges, breaks, reinforcing activities such as use of the computer, puzzle games, and free reading time.
- Contracts and token economies
- Mystery awards
- Public recognition class-wide, school-wide, and community-wide
- Use of a menu of reinforcers. The students may contribute to the list with guidance from the teacher. The list may include use of computer, free reading, catch-up time on assignments, and games.
- Reinforcement menus for short-term and long-term rewards. Short-term reinforcers are those that can be immediately applied such as games, breaks, and free reading. Long-term reinforcers can be delayed such as a pizza party, movie, or an extra recess.

- Use combinations of positive consequences such as social praise followed by a privilege. For example, "Michael, you have done a wonderful job with your math. Congratulations. You can spend some time on the computer now."
- Be sure to explain the procedures on the first day of class and provide reminders throughout the year.

Using Negative Consequences

While positive consequences should be your primary response toward behavior, negative consequences have an important role. Specifically, negative consequences communicate to students that problem behavior is unacceptable. In other words, negative consequences help to teach limits of behavior. There are five important rules for using negative consequences:

1. Deliver the consequences consistently at each occurrence of problem behavior.

2. Use only mild consequences.

3. Apply negative consequences in conjunction with positive consequences. That is, if negative consequences are applied then you need to be ready to apply positive consequences at the earliest opportunity.

4. Maintain a ratio of positive to negative consequences of at least 3:1.

5. Maintain the student's respect and dignity when delivering negative consequences.

Examples of negative consequences for problem behavior are:

- Loss of teacher attention and approval
- Loss of privileges
- Time out or removal from an activity
- Restitution where the student is required to provide some service or help to make up for the problems he or she caused
- Isolation

- Response cost where a student loses points or minutes of free time
- Parent contact and conferences

Become very familiar with school policies and procedures for serious behavior. Take time to determine the school policy and procedures for:

1. Which behaviors warrant office referrals.

2. Completing the office referral form.

3. Sending a student to the office.

4. Your responsibilities in the office referral process.

In addition, make sure you are very familiar with the school crisis and emergency procedures (such as student possession of weapons).

Instructional Management Techniques

Teachers can prevent a number of problem behaviors by paying careful attention to establishing classroom expectations and by consistently applying consequences. Review the following topics in Chapter 5, Managing Instruction, as strategies for intervening during instruction to prevent problem behavior that may occur during the course of the school day.

- Establish an entry activity.
- Secure everyone's attention before beginning explanations.
- Plan for difficult transitions.
- Use direct speech.
- Avoid dead time.
- Settle students down near the end of each period.
- Keep initial explanations brief.

In addition, the following strategies are important in preventing problem behavior:

Serve as a role model. Students respond well to good role models. Some students do not have good role models in their lives, so contact with the classroom teacher meets this important need. For example, if you want the students to work quietly, then you should talk quietly and avoid raising your voice. If you want the children to respect each other, then you should show respect to them and avoid putting them down or embarrassing them.

Frequently acknowledge cooperative students. Perhaps the most powerful strategy for implementing classroom expectations is to frequently reinforce students who exhibit appropriate behaviors. This procedure calls attention to the appropriate behavior and provides a model for the rest of the class. Whenever possible, acknowledge the positive, cooperative behavior of students who may have behavior problems. Develop procedures or structures to remind yourself of the need to frequently look for students who are displaying the expected behaviors. For example, write notes in lesson plans, daily planners, or on a special place on the chalkboard.

The following procedures are helpful for reinforcing expected behavior:

- Watch for opportunities to praise students for their special efforts or for cooperative behavior. Recognize students who show desirable behavior.

- Distinguish between praise for cooperation and praise for acquisition of instructional skill. Both forms of achievement need to be equally acknowledged.

- Make contact with all students. Some students are more visible than others and naturally receive more teacher attention; a special effort is usually necessary to make contact with all students. As a result, students with problem behavior may eventually learn that they have the same chance of receiving teacher attention through their positive, cooperative behavior as through their inappropriate behavior.

Establish systematic correction procedures for problem behavior. Provide careful explanations of the importance of following classroom rules. However, it is not sufficient, by itself, to ensure that the rules will be followed.

Design a correction plan that contains a series of steps in which the least intrusive step is used first and more intrusive measures come into play only if the problem behavior persists. For example:

1. Remove attention from the student who is displaying inappropriate behavior, and acknowledge other students nearby who are exhibiting the expected behavior.

2. Redirect the student to the expected behavior with a gesture or verbal prompt, cite the classroom rule being violated, and be sure to acknowledge subsequent cooperation and displays of expected behavior by the student.

3. Secure the student's attention and clearly inform him or her of the expected behavior, provide immediate opportunities for practice, and acknowledge the changed behavior when it occurs.

4. Deliver a brief warning by providing an opportunity for the student to choose between displaying the expected behavior and experiencing a penalty or loss of privilege.

5. Deliver the penalty or loss of privilege in a matter-of-fact matter (for example, timeout or loss of some recess time), and do not argue with the student about details of the penalty.

Catch problems early. Act quickly at the onset of inappropriate behavior and immediately begin the appropriate correction procedures specified earlier. In this way: (1) Students learn that the teacher is serious about implementing the expected behaviors; (2) The behavior may be prevented from escalating; and (3) The procedure may prevent other students from joining in with the inappropriate behavior.

Maintain attentive student behavior by frequently scanning the whole class and not turning your back to the students for lengthy periods. If possible, other staff should be used to assist slower students or to keep the body of the class working in an independent activity so additional attention may be given to individual students as necessary.

Act quickly if students are engaging in activities that involve: (1) Missing equipment; (2) Threats to the safety of others; and (3) Changing a prescribed activity.

The most effective strategies for quickly addressing problem behavior require directly attending to the students who are cooperative and academically engaged and redirecting those who are not. If further consequences are necessary, they should be delivered in a brief manner. Remember not to lecture or give lengthy explanations. In this process, simply state the rule infraction and the corresponding consequence that is associated with it.

Attention

You can safely assume that many problem behaviors are driven by the students' need for attention or control. Unfortunately, problem behavior is more likely to get staff attention than good behavior. There are three ways that students may get attention:

1. By exhibiting good behavior they may earn reinforcement such as approval, privileges, or recognition.

2. By exhibiting problem behavior they may receive punishment such as reprimands, time-outs, office referrals, or loss of privileges.

3. By receiving noncontingent attention in which the teacher provides attention through greetings, jobs, visits, or sharing interests.

> **RULE**
>
> The ratio of attention delivered for good behavior and through non-contingent attention should exceed the attention for problem behavior by at least 3:1.

Precorrection

On the basis of your experience with other students and with certain individual students you can often predict student behavior. In other words, you can anticipate their behavior under specific conditions. For example, when Sarah is asked to correct her work she refuses, folds her arms, and starts to complain. With precorrection you make adjustments beforehand to headoff the problem behavior. These adjustments include reminders, behavioral rehearsal, modifications of the task, supervision changes, changes in routines, and setting changes.

Behavioral Momentum

When you know the conditions that set off student behavior you can engage the student in easy or preferred tasks just before the difficult setting or task is introduced. In other words, get the student "going" before starting on the harder task. In this way the student is already cooperating and succeeding and is more likely to attempt the difficult task. Be sure to follow the hard task with an easy or reinforcing activity. For example, begin the math class with examples the students have mastered, then introduce the newer problems that are more difficult, and finish with one problem example they have mastered.

Active Supervision

Active supervision is a critical skill for preventing and managing student behavior, particularly in settings where (a) large groups of students are involved such as recess, cafeteria, school entry and exit, and bus loading and unloading; and (b) during transitions such as from class to lunch or from recess to class. The keys to active supervision are to:

1. Know the rules and procedures required of you and the students.

2. Be first to the site and last to leave.

3. Move around and vary your position.

4. Interact at a high rate with the students (greet, acknowledge, chat, reinforce, and correct).

5. Use proximity control (the closer you are to students the more likely they are to cooperate).

6. Scan all areas frequently, especially trouble spots and distant areas.

7. Catch problems early.

Summary

As the diversity of classrooms increases dramatically, teachers face accelerating pressures to teach and manage their students effectively. In addition, one of the many challenges teachers must address is the increasing complexity of the social-behavioral problems children and youth bring to school.

This chapter recommended the use of prevention procedures as a first step related to the design and proper functioning of the classroom environment. By systematically using these strategies, students are provided with a stable, predictable environment that will generally encourage desirable behavior and minimize problem behavior. Some students, of course, will be unresponsive to these proactive procedures that are applied to all students. In these instances, even the most optimally designed and operating classroom won't help to maintain appropriate behavior in the students with problem behavior. It may be necessary to provide more individualized instruction on academics, classroom routines, and behavioral instruction as described in earlier chapters. In addition, there are strategic steps that can be taken to address problem behavior after it occurs. This information is presented in the next chapter.

Managing the Full Range of
Problem Behavior

THE PREVIOUS CHAPTER presented strategies for preventing problem behavior. However, there is always the likelihood that problem behavior will emerge. Moreover, these behaviors of concern may range from minor behaviors, such as out-of-seat, to serious behavior, such as fighting or assault. This chapter discusses six steps for addressing this full range of behavior problems: (1) Categories of problem behavior; (2) Strategies for managing minor problem behavior; (3) Strategies for preventing escalating behavior; (4) Office referrals; (5) Crisis management procedures; and (6) Follow-up procedures.

Categories of Problem Behavior

In most schools, problem behavior is identified as either a minor infraction (i.e., behavior that is managed immediately by staff) or a serious school violation (i.e., behavior that involves an office referral and management by an administrator). Table 11 shows how schools generally categorize the full range of problem behavior.

TABLE 11

CATEGORIES OF PROBLEM BEHAVIOR

1. *Minor school infractions* are defined as relatively mild behaviors that are disruptive to the teaching and learning process and can easily escalate into more serious behavior problems. Common examples include being tardy for class, talking too loudly in the hallways, not having materials for class, and skipping school (truancy). These behaviors are typically managed immediately and quickly by staff in the context in which the behavior occurs.

2. *Serious school violations* are not law infractions, but represent serious breaches of school rules and behavior that seriously disrupts school functioning. These include, for example, sustained noncompliance and defiance, verbal abuse toward staff, low levels of physical aggression, vandalism, and chronic (repeated) minor infractions. These behaviors typically warrant an office referral and are managed by the administration (or designee) or a team of teachers and other staff members.

3. *Illegal behavior* refers to actual violations of the law. Examples include possession of weapons or controlled substances, theft, assault, vandalism, and intimidation. This list should be confirmed with local law enforcement agencies and district policies. These behaviors typically warrant office referrals and are managed by the administration (or designee) in conjunction with local law enforcement agents.

The teacher must become very familiar with behaviors that they are expected to address (minor problem behavior) and behavior that warrants an office referral.

Strategies for Managing Minor Problem Behavior

If you act in a timely and effective manner at the first sign of problem behavior, you can interrupt the behavior before it becomes serious. There are two steps in the process:

1. Recognize the early onset of problem behavior. The indicators usually take the form of off-task behavior, low level noise or disruption, talking out, out-of-seat, and other attention-seeking behavior.

2. Use effective strategies for disrupting the problem behavior and redirecting the student toward appropriate behavior.

Strategies for interrupting problem behavior are:

Planned Ignoring—Many students exhibit problem behavior to get teacher attention. When the teacher ignores problem behavior and simultaneously attends to students who exhibit expected behavior, the students may learn that if they want teacher attention then they need to exhibit good behavior.

Redirection—In this strategy simply focus on the task at hand. Prompt the task or redirect the student to the task. For example, if the student is out of his or her seat, simply say, "It is math time now," and point to the student's seat. In this way you are providing attention to the task at hand versus attending directly to the problem behavior.

Use of Gestures and Signals—Use nonverbal gestures and signals to prompt the student or students to the task. For example, put a finger to your lips to signal quiet down, and point to the desk to signal return to your desk. Use a class signal to obtain a group response. For example, flick the lights on and off to signal everyone to sit down and be quiet. Or hold up five fingers signaling the students have five seconds to be in their seats and quiet.

Managing Agitation—Agitation is a behavioral term that includes emotional dispositions such as being upset, angry, depressed, worried, anxious, fearful, and frustrated. When students become agitated they are not only difficult to teach and manage, but their behavior may escalate to more serious problems. Agitation is a sign of more serious behavior. The basic approach to managing agitation is to: (1) Recognize the signs of student agitation; and (2) Use techniques to reduce the agitation.

1. Signs of Agitation—Agitation is manifested by both increases and decreases in behavior. Table 12 shows agitated behavior of students that is representative of increases and decreases in behavior.

TABLE 12

INCREASES IN BEHAVIOR	DECREASES IN BEHAVIOR
• Darting eyes • Nonconversational language • Busy hands • Moving in and out of groups • Off-task, then on-task behavior • Starting and stopping activities • Moving around the room	• Staring into space • Subdued language • Contained hands • Lack in interaction and involvement in activities • Withdrawal from groups and activities • Lack of responding • Veiled eyes

2. Techniques for Managing Agitation—Once the student's agitated behavior has been recognized, the primary goal is to use strategies to calm the student down and assist him or her to become engaged with the present classroom activity. Because these strategies are supportive in nature, they must be implemented *before* the onset of serious behavioral episodes; otherwise, there is the risk that the chain of inappropriate behavior may be reinforced. The critical issue is timing. The techniques should be implemented at the earliest indications of agitation. The techniques are listed in Table 13.

TABLE 13

TECHNIQUES FOR MANAGING AGITATION	
Teacher Support	Communicate that you recognize that the student is having a problem.
Space	Provide the student with an opportunity to have some isolation from the rest of the class.
Choices	Give the student some choices or options.
Preferred Activities	Allow the student to engage in a preferred activity for a short period of time to help him or her focus.
Teacher Proximity	Move near or stand near the student.
Independent Activities	Engage the student in independent activities to provide isolation.
Movement Activities	Use activities and tasks that require movement such as errands, cleaning the chalkboard, and distributing papers.
Involvement of the Student	Where possible, involve the student in the plan. In this way there is more chance of ownership and generalization to other settings.
Relaxation Activities	Use audiotapes, drawing activities, breathing and relaxation techniques.

Strategies for Preventing Escalating Behavior

While it is clear that serious behavior warrants an office referral, there are occasions when the student behavior starts out as minor behavior and escalates into serious behavior. The basic approaches to preventing escalating behavior are to: (1) Recognize the behavioral signs for escalation; (2) Avoid escalating responses; (3) Maintain calmness, respect, and detachment; and (4) Use crisis prevention techniques.

Behavioral Signs of Escalation

At this point the student's behavior is typically focused and directed toward someone. The behavior is often assured a predictable and rapid response from the teacher (or others). In other words, students exhibit engaging behaviors such as:

- Questioning and arguing
- Noncompliance and defiance
- Off-task behavior
- Provocation of others
- Compliance with accompanying inappropriate behavior
- Criterion problems
- Limit testing
- Whining and crying
- Avoidance and escape
- Threats and intimidation
- Verbal abuse
- Interference with others
- Disruption
- Destruction of property

Avoid Escalating Responses

Typically an escalating pattern involves the student exhibiting problem behavior, staff responding to this behavior, then the student exhibiting more serious behavior. The first step for staff is to avoid responding in a way that will escalate the student. The following behaviors are common escalating responses and should be avoided by staff:

- Agitated behavior from staff such as shouting
- Cornering the student
- Tugging or grabbing the student
- Engaging in power struggles
- Getting "in the student's face"
- Discrediting the student

- Nagging or "preaching"
- Arguing

Maintain Calmness, Respect, and Detachment

When teachers approach students in the context of problem behavior there is always the chance that the students may escalate their behavior. The teacher's behavior at this point needs to be controlled and nonjudgmental. Some guidelines for approaching students in more dangerous or volatile situations are:

- Move slowly and deliberately toward the problem area.
- Speak privately to the involved students.
- Speak calmly using a flat, controlled voice.
- Minimize body language and avoid crowding the students.
- Keep a reasonable distance.
- Speak respectfully.
- Establish eye level contact if possible.
- Use language that is brief, simple, and direct.
- Stay with the agenda and do not be sidetracked.
- Withdraw if the problems escalate and follow the school emergency procedures.
- Acknowledge cooperation if the students disengage and follow directions.

Use Crisis Prevention Techniques

These strategies are designed to interrupt the chain of escalating behavior or to provide an ultimatum to a student who is persisting with problem behavior. There are three steps in this strategy:

1. *Establish a negative consequence beforehand.* Typical negative consequences for problem behavior include office referral, detention, suspension, police call, and parent call. The consequence should be approved by proper authorities and explained to students before it is implemented.

2. *Deliver the information in a nonconfrontational manner.* Information is delivered to the students by:

   a. Presenting the expected behavior and the negative consequence as a choice or decision for the student to make.

   b. Allowing some time for the student to decide.

   c. Withdrawing from the student, attending to other students, or engaging in some other task.

   Example: "Michael, you are asked to return to your desk or I will send for the principal." (Decision) "You have a few seconds to decide." (Time) The teacher then moves to the other students. (Withdrawal).

3. *Follow through.* Action taken by the teacher in following through is determined by the choice the student makes on whether to follow the expected behavior or to maintain the problem behavior.

   a. If the student chooses the expected behavior, acknowledge the choice briefly, and continue with the lesson or activity.

   b. If the student does not choose the expected behavior, that is, maintains the problem behavior, deliver the negative consequence.

   c. If the student chooses the expected behavior after the allotted time has elapsed, deliver the negative consequence.

   d. Conduct a debriefing session. The teacher visits with the student later that day to review the incident, problem-solve, and help the student to decide how to manage this situation in the future.

Office Referrals

Teachers are expected to make office referrals for student behavior that is quite serious. These behaviors were identified in the first section of this chapter under Categories of Behavior. It is very important for the teacher to become fluent and familiar with office referral procedures. The reason is that the administrator relies on this information to make decisions on what action to take regarding the student's infraction. Pay close attention to the following guidelines listed in Table 14 when making office referrals.

TABLE 14

GUIDELINES IN MAKING OFFICE REFERRALS
1. Be sure that the behavior warrants an office referral (i.e., that the behavior is on the list of serious behaviors that should be referred to the office).
2. Complete the office referral form in full. Remember, the administrator uses the information to make a decision, and the details are usually entered in the recordkeeping data base.
3. Follow the procedures for sending the student to the office (i.e., whether the student is escorted, or whether the office is notified that a student has been referred).
4. Complete the form in a timely manner. Ensure the form reaches the administrator before he or she has to visit with the student.
5. Be available to provide more information as needed.

Crisis Management Procedures

One of the most difficult responsibilities facing teachers is managing student crisis behavior. Crisis or emergency situations include a stranger in the building; bomb threat; explosion; serious injury; death; serious fight; drug dealing on campus; weapon possession; natural disasters; kidnapping; hostage taking; and student, staff or other out-of-control and violent behavior. These crisis events may be life threatening and seriously impact on the safety of others, have liability issues, significantly disrupt class, and may cause extreme emotional strain on staff and students. For these reasons teachers must be very knowledgeable of and fluent with procedures for managing crisis behavior.

Take active steps to become very familiar with the procedures. You should not be in a position to create steps for managing crisis behavior. The steps are analogous to fire drills, in that teachers and students know exactly what to do when the fire alarm sounds. It is not within the scope of this book to delineate procedures for managing crisis behavior. It is understood that the school district and school have written policies and procedures on crisis management. Table 15 presents the general steps typically followed by teachers in a crisis management plan.

TABLE 15

GENERAL CRISIS MANAGEMENT STEPS
1. Assess the situation to determine the gravity or potential risk.
2. Call or send for help.
3. Monitor the situation, make attempts to verbally defuse the situation if appropriate, control the crowd, and wait for help from experts.
4. Step aside when help comes and let them take over.
5. Follow up as needed such as submitting a report.

Remember, we cannot assume that schools are safe places anymore. Be sure to follow the school protocol to the letter for managing crisis or emergency events.

Follow-Up Procedures

The purpose of the follow-up procedures is to prevent the problem behavior from arising again. The basic approach is one of problem solving. Essentially, the teacher helps the students identify the problem, recognize their inappropriate response, and determine what options they have should these circumstances arise again. The features of a follow-up procedure are:

- Select a time where you and the student can meet briefly and privately.

- Use a set format with key questions such as: What did you do? Why did you do it? What will you do next time that would be acceptable?

- Assist the student to identify the triggers and events leading up to the serious behavior.

- Assist the student to pinpoint where he or she could have averted a crisis situation.

- Assist the student to select an alternative response for the problem situation.

- Assist the student to make a commitment to behave differently next time this situation arises.

- Assure the student of your confidence that he or she can be successful.

Summary

Teachers are increasingly faced with managing a full range of problem behavior, from minor disruptive behavior to serious, life threatening behavior in the classroom. Most problem behavior can be averted by paying careful attention to the details of classroom instruction and organization. However, behavior concerns will arise. There are no shortcuts for managing these behaviors. Teachers should adopt a systematic approach that involves using strategies to establish desirable behavior and developing procedures for managing crises. Also, if the problem behavior is not changing, strategies need to be modified. In this way the teacher will be able to establish a safe and positive environment for learning and spend more time teaching and less time on managing problem behavior.

chapter 7

> Taking Charge Beyond
> the Classroom

TEACHERS ARE OFTEN identified by their classrooms. In one sense this is where the teacher spends most of his or her time and where most responsibilities lie. This does not mean, though, that the classroom functions as an island. Rather, in a successful classroom the teacher works closely with other staff and pays careful attention to settings outside the classroom. This chapter addresses details that enable the teacher to work effectively with: (1) All key staff; and (2) School settings outside the classroom.

Working With Key Staff and Other Personnel

One of the most significant trends in modern education is the need for staff to work together. Hiring procedures for teachers place high priority on the "team player" concept and interpersonal skills. In an ideal school, staff work together in a constructive manner, support each other, respect each other's work, and contribute to the overall program. A high level of staff collaboration helps to produce a stable and consistent environment for their students. Students then experience a certain level of structure and predictability throughout their school day regardless of where they are in the building. In addition, when staff work effectively together, they are more likely to support each other professionally and emotionally. Effective support and communication between staff help to strengthen morale and lead to a positive learning environment for their students. For example, when there is effective communication and support between the classroom teacher and the physical education teacher, the students are clearer on expectations at each setting. The classroom teacher ensures that the students are on time and prepared for the physical education class. Similarly, the physical education teacher has the students ready to return to the classroom on time and orderly. Also, the physical education teacher turns in the grades to the classroom teacher in a timely manner with adequate explanations. In other words, the classroom teacher and the physical education teacher work effectively together.

The classroom teacher also has to work effectively with other personnel besides colleagues in the school. These personnel include substitute teachers, volunteers, and parents. There are three major steps designed to assist a classroom teacher to work effectively with other people who have responsibilities with their students. These steps are: (1) Identify the key personnel who have responsibilities with the class; (2) Develop a communication system; and (3) Identify the specific procedures in working with other personnel where necessary. The primary goal is to develop a system that minimizes interruptions to you and your work with the students. The extremes are to never communicate with other personnel because of the disruptions it may cause (which ultimately penalizes the student's learning and progress), or to develop a communication system that is too intrusive, takes too much time away from the class, and limits the students' opportunities to learn. The solution lies in having a system that is effective, efficient, and mutually acceptable.

Identify the Key Personnel

The classroom teacher typically has to collaborate, at some level, with many personnel. The first step is to make a list of key personnel who have involvement with your students. The following list is typical:

- Administration
- Specialist teachers (such as art, music, physical education, media teachers)

- Team teachers
- Special education and Chapter I teachers
- School nurse
- Paraprofessionals
- Substitute teachers
- Volunteers
- Parents
- Guest speakers and presenters
- Agency representatives (for example, youth corrections and child protection services)
- Other

Develop a Communication System

It is absolutely critical to develop a communication system that not only works for you but works for other personnel. The system needs to be efficient as neither you nor other personnel have "surplus time." Some guidelines for an effective and efficient communication system are:

Identify the schedule of contact that is needed. Teachers typically have the need to connect with other staff and personnel: (1) On a regular or fixed basis (daily, weekly, or monthly; (2) Intermittently (once a week or once a month; (3) As needed (for example, a meeting may be called if there are problems or signs of problems); and (4) On an emergency basis (procedures are in place so contact can be made in the case of crises or emergencies).

Choose the kind of contact to be used. There are many ways in which a teacher may connect with other personnel. Standard procedures include visits, meetings, phone calls, letters, notes, forms, and electronic mail. Again, choose what works for you and the other person.

Identify Specific Procedures for Working With Other Personnel

Once a list of key personnel has been identified and a communication system established, the next step is to identify the critical or unique responsibilities of other personnel and your specific role. The overall process is to identify the specific responsibilities of other personnel and then to become familiar with the procedures for working with these personnel. It is helpful to develop a set of key questions to ask these personnel such as:

1. What are the major responsibilities of other staff personnel that directly affect your responsibilities?

2. What do you, the classroom teacher, need to do in order to meet your responsibilities in working effectively with other personnel?

3. What are the major responsibilities of other staff personnel that directly affect your students?

4. How do you need to prepare your students to maximize the services or role of other personnel in their work that affects your students?

5. What written products are available that specify the roles and responsibilites for your work with other staff?

6. What paperwork, forms, and reports are needed from you for working with other staff?

In Table 16 some of the typical roles and responsibilities for staff personnel are listed along with the corresponding role and responsibilities for the classroom teacher. Classroom teachers are encouraged to develop their own list with more specific roles and responsibilities as needed.

TABLE 16: Responsibilities of Key Personnel and the Role of the Classroom Teacher

ROLES AND RESPONSIBILITIES OF OTHER PERSONNEL	ROLES AND RESPONSIBILITIES OF THE CLASSROOM TEACHER

Administration
  School discipline
  Parent/teacher meetings
  Teacher evaluations
  Develop resources as appropriate
	Know protocol for office referrals
	Know protocol
	Know procedures and expectations
	Utilize as appropriate

Specialist Teachers
  Provide specialist instruction
  Coordinate schedule
  Conduct special events
	Provide support and respect
	Teach routines and transition behavior
	Cooperate with schedule

Special Education and Chapter Staff
  Provide additional assistance to
    students as needed
  Manage documentation
  Administer testing
  Coordinate schedule for services
	Know protocol
	Provide requested information in a
	  timely manner
	Assist where appropriate
	Cooperate with schedule and teach
	students procedures

Paraprofessionals
  Specific assignments
  Supervisory responsibilities
	Provide support and respect
	Ensure student respect
	Cooperate with schedule and duties
	Know specific needs (e.g., breaks and
	  duty-free lunch)
	Cooperate with contract and do not take
	  advantage of their own time

School Nurse
  Schoolwide checks and programs
  Specific protocol for visits
  Provision of health care
	Know protocol for visits
	Know student entry and exit procedures
	Know paperwork requirements
	Honor schedule

(continued)

ROLES AND RESPONSIBILITIES OF OTHER PERSONNEL	ROLES AND RESPONSIBILITIES OF THE CLASSROOM TEACHER
Parents Partners in child's education Important ally Provider of consistency and support	Develop clear communication procedures Ensure parents know how and when to contact you Collaborate as much as possible Develop reporting system Encourage and support where possible
Service Agencies Additional services Advocate for student rights Assist with outside school activities and responsibilities	Know and follow protocol Cooperate and work as collaboratively as possible Attend to paperwork thoroughly and in a timely manner Develop communication system
Volunteers Provide "extra hands" Serve as tutors for needy students Assist with clerical work Assist with special activities	Define role and responsibilities Support and respect Provide training as necessary Express gratitude personally and from students
Substitute Teachers Critical role in replacing teachers on leave for staff development, sickness Part of faculty Provide continuity for students	Provide support and respect Know and follow protocol Develop clear communication lines Have necessary work well prepared and well organized Prepare students for substitutes Follow up on student behavior toward substitutes

Managing School Settings Outside the Classroom

Teachers have responsibilities for their students wherever they are in the school setting. While they may not be responsible for supervision, they do have responsibilities for their students' behavior. For example, teachers like to hear that their students are always on time for lunch and behave very well in the lunch room. By contrast, teachers do not like to hear that their class is often late for lunch and is the most unruly class in the lunch room. In some cases teachers can be very effective when called on to help with some of their students who may be having problems in other settings. Similarly, teachers can be particularly helpful to other supervising staff by carefully preparing their students for transitions and expected behavior in the next setting. For example, the students are more likely to behave on the bus if the teacher has the students settled at the end of the period, briefly reminds them of the bus rules, and plans for an orderly exit to the bus pick-up area. In all, it is in everyone's best interest—the students, supervising staff, the teachers themselves, and the whole school—for teachers to play an active role in managing the behavior of their students in settings outside the classroom. This chapter identifies the specific steps for teacher's to address in managing their students in other school settings. These steps are: (1) Provide an overall expectation for student behavior outside the classroom; (2) Identify important school settings outside the classroom; (3) Teach the behavior expectations for each setting; (4) Develop a monitoring and feedback system; (5) Develop a specific plan for students who have problems; and (6) Develop a periodic review system with the class.

Provide an Overall Expectation for Student Behavior Outside the Classroom

Address this topic during the first day of the school year and review periodically throughout the year. Remind the class that they are not only expected to follow rules in the classroom, but they are to follow the school rules wherever they are, whether they are in the cafeteria, the library, at recess, or on the bus. Also emphasize that even though someone else may be supervising these areas, students will be accountable to you if there are problems. You might explain to them, "It is just like a family; even though you are not at home your parents care about your behavior outside your home. For example, your parents would be very concerned if you misbehaved at someone else's home or downtown, and they would more than likely take action. It is the same at school." You might then say, "Here is how it works. I am your teacher and I expect good behavior from you everywhere in the school. I will take time to explain the behaviors in other settings in the school and will follow up on how you are doing."

Identify Important School Setting Outside the Classroom

Make a list and even put together a folder for the major settings in the school that have specific behavior expectations. Sometimes this information is available in a staff or student handbook. If a handbook is not available, develop one for yourself.

The typical major settings are:

- Cafeteria
- Recess
- Hallways
- Restrooms
- School bus
- Before and after school
- Library
- Gym

Collect the following information about each setting:

- Behavioral expectations for the students
- Specific routines
- Arrival and departure times
- Specific responsibilities of the teacher (e.g., where he or she delivers the class; where and when the class is picked up)
- Traffic patterns (e.g., which hallways or doors are used)

Teach the Behavior Expectations for Each Setting

To teach the behavioral expectations for other school settings, use the same strategies presented in Chapter 2 for teaching routines. Essentially, the basic teaching steps are to:

- Carefully explain the rules and expectations. Emphasize the specific expectations such as quiet in the library; orderliness, cleanliness, and manners in the cafeteria.

- Provide opportunities for practice. Actually walk the students through the procedures and routines where possible such as for cafeteria behavior.

- Monitor student performance (or develop a feedback system with the supervisor).

- Review student performance with the class.

- Conduct these teaching plans just prior to the first time the students encounter the specific setting during the first week of school.

Develop a Monitoring and Feedback System

Even though the teacher may carefully prepare the students for settings outside the classroom, there is no guarantee that the students will follow the rules. Or, the students may start out well, but as time goes on their behavior may deteriorate. One way to prevent these problems and to ensure good behavior in these other settings is to develop a monitoring system. Clearly, if the teacher is responsible for supervision in these settings, the monitoring system is automatically in place. However, in most cases other staff are responsible for the supervision. In these cases there are three strategies for developing a monitoring system:

1. Develop a feedback system between you and the supervisor. For example, the supervisor in the cafeteria could send a note or complete a standard form on how the class performed.

2. Visit the setting on a periodic basis to see firsthand how the students are behaving.

3. Visit informally with the supervisor. You could simply ask, "How is my class doing at recess? Any problems?"

Note: It is very important that you obtain information early regarding problems. You can then act quickly to address the problems.

Develop a Specific Plan for Students Who Have Problems

It is not uncommon for individual students to have problems in settings outside the classroom (even though they may follow the rules in the classroom). There are many reasons for this apparent inconsistency. There is often less structure, more students, more space, fewer staff per students, and fewer things to do in the setting compared to the classroom. These students should be quickly identified through the monitoring and feedback system. The teacher can be of immeasurable help in changing these students' behavior. Usually there are three steps the teacher can take to address the problem:

1. Provide a stronger focus before the student enters the setting. Just before the student leaves the class, take him or her aside and go over the rules and provide encouragement. The student could be required to state the rules or write the rules as a form of rehearsal.

2. Provide closer supervision and feedback. Ask the supervisor to provide information on how the student performs. For example, the supervisor could give the student some form of "report" to take to class such as a green card for good behavior or a red card to indicate problems.

3. Conduct a brief review of the students' performance based on the feedback from the supervisor. Consequences could be delivered such as a positive consequence for good behavior or a negative consequence for problem behavior.

Note: If there are several students from one class having problems, then more teaching may be required for the whole class. Provide more rehearsal, more supervision, and more feedback.

Summary

In an effective school the role of the teacher extends beyond the classroom. Teachers need to work closely with key staff in the school. If other staff members are involved with the classroom, the teacher develops procedures to work effectively with these staff members. Moreover, they play a critical role in preparing their students for other school settings and in following up on their students' behavior. In this way the classroom teacher can be of immeasurable help to other teachers, staff, and supervisors, and will help to provide consistency for his or her students that will have positive effects on their learning.

Getting Off to a Good Start

THE WAY IN which the school year begins dictates how the year will proceed. The sooner students are focused and productively engaged in learning activities the more likely they are to maintain and improve these behaviors through the year. The opposite is also true. A slow and unplanned start may lead to disorder, limited learning, and high rates of problem behavior.

The purpose of this final chapter is to present a number of checklists, derived from the topics presented in this book, to assist the teacher in covering critical bases at the start of the school year. These checklists are designed to serve as guidelines so the teacher can develop his or her own specific checklists.

CHECKLIST 1

DESIGNING THE PHYSICAL ARRANGEMENT OF THE CLASSROOM		
Activity	Completion Date	Notes
1. Locate specific classroom areas for: a. Independent work b. Group work c. Free activity d. Time out e. Materials storage f. Notice board g. Quiet area h. Other 2. Draw up seating plans: a. Rows b. Clusters c. Semicircular d. Other 3. Identify other classroom design tasks: _____ _____ _____ _____		

The Effective Elementary Classroom

CHECKLIST 2

PLANNING THE CURRICULA		
Activity	**Completion Date**	**Notes**
1. List classroom subjects: a. b. c. d. e. f.		
2. Develop timelines for each subject.		
3. Design modules (6-week) for each subject.		
4. Assemble materials for each module.		
5. Develop activities for each module.		
6. Identify testing procedures for each subject.		
7. Assemble materials for each test.		
8. Review student records.		
9. List student groupings.		

CHECKLIST 3

DEVELOPING AND COORDINATING SCHEDULES		
Activity	**Completion Date**	**Notes**
1. Identify school-wide fixed schedules for: a. Start of school day b. Morning recess c. Lunch d. Afternoon recess e. Other		
2. Identify specialists' schedule: a. Music b. Art c. Library d. Physical education e. Labs f. Other		
3. Identify team teaching periods.		
4. Develop classroom schedule for: a. Master schedule b. First day c. First week d. First month		

CHECKLIST 4

DESIGNING CLASSROOM ROUTINES		
Subject	Completion Date	Notes
1. List classroom routines to be established: a. b. c. d. e. f. g.		
2. Schedule routines to be taught: a. First day b. First week c. First month		
3. Develop procedures for teaching classroom routines.		

CHECKLIST 5

SETTING CLASSROOM BEHAVIORAL EXPECTATIONS		
Subject	Completion Date	Notes
1. Identify classroom expectations: a. b. c. d. e.		
2. Develop schedule for teaching behavioral expectations: a. First day b. First week c. First month		
3. Develop procedures for teaching behavioral expectations.		
4. Develop procedures for communicating behavioral expectations: a. Classroom display b. Parents c. Other		
5. Develop simple discipline plan.		
6. Develop list of positive consequences.		
7. Develop procedures for negative consequences.		
8. Other.		

The Effective Elementary Classroom

CHECKLIST 6

PROCEDURES FOR WORKING WITH OTHERS		
Subject	Completion Date	Notes
1. List key staff who have responsibilities with class.		
2. Develop communication system for each key staff member.		
3. Identify procedures for working with each staff member.		
4. Other.		

CHECKLIST 7

PROCEDURES FOR COVERING SETTINGS OUTSIDE THE CLASSROOM		
Subject	Completion Date	Notes
1. Establish expectations for student behavior outside the classroom.		
2. Identify major school settings outside the classroom.		
3. Identify specific behaviors for major settings.		
4. Implement teaching plan for behaviors in each setting.		
5. Develop monitoring and feedback system.		
6. Develop specific plan for students with recurring problem behavior.		
7. Develop system for periodic review with class.		

In closing, here are a few "tricks of the trade" from some effective teachers:

- Visit students' homes.
- Write a letter to students with an opening day activity assigned.
- Use "get to know you" games, interactions, songs.
- Provide classroom and building tours.
- Let students brainstorm their class rules, narrow them down to four or five important ones, then revise them into classroom code for all to sign.
- Use introductory listening skill activities.
- Demonstrate and role play classroom/school expectations for the first six weeks and revisit as often as needed.
- Offer a "Self-Manager Button" as an incentive for responsible and appropriate behavior that all students are capable of earning and working toward throughout the year.
- Overemphasize and praise students who are doing things correctly/ positively.
- Hold class meetings to allow student input and peer pressure to guide class in a positive direction. (Charney, 1992)
- Start off slowly and review daily routines until students show a comfort level.
- Post a daily schedule.
- Know where everything is such as building facilities and supplies.
- Have classroom rules posted—the discipline plan should be clearly understood.
- Have name tags on desks and/or students.
- Do lots of modeling of appropriate behavior as well as things like how to write headings on student papers.
- Have a plan for parent involvement—have a sign-up sheet in the classroom on the first day.

References

Becker, W.C. (1986). *Applied psychology for teachers: A behavioral cognitive approach*. Chicago, IL: Science Research Associates.

Charney, R.S. (1992). *Teaching children to care: Management in the responsive classroom*. Pittsfield, MA: Eagle Printing, Bindery and Mailing.

Engelmann, S. & Bruner, E. (1983). *Reading mastery, Level I, DISTAR Reading*. Chicago, IL: Science Research Associates.

Gamoran, A. (1992). Is ability grouping equitable? *Educational leadership, 50* (2), 11-17.

Sugai, G. & Tindal, G. (1993). *Effective school consultation: An interactive approach*. Pacific Grove, CA: Brooks/Cole.

Walker, H., Colvin, G., & Ramsey, E. (1995). *Antisocial behavior in school: Strategies and best practices*. Pacific Grove, CA: Brooks/Cole.

Bibliography

Cangelosi, J. (1988). *Classroom management strategies: Gaining and maintaining students' cooperation.* White Plains, NY: Longman.

Colvin, G. (1992). *Managing acting-out behavior: A staff development program to prevent and manage acting-out behavior* [Video program]. Eugene, OR: Behavior Associates.

Cummings, C. (1989). *Managing to teach* (3rd ed.). Edmonds, WA: Teaching Inc.

Evertson, C.M., Emmer, E.T., Clements, B.S., Sanford, J.P., & Worsham. (1984). *Classroom management for elementary teachers.* Englewood Cliffs, NJ: Prentice-Hall.

Hofmeister, A. & Lubke, M. (1990). *Research into practice: Implementing effective teaching practices.* Boston, MA: Allyn and Bacon.

Johnson, D.W. & Johnson, R. (1985). Classroom conflict: Controversy versus debate in learning groups. *American Educational Research Journal.* 22 (2), 237-256.

Johnson, D.W., Johnson, R.T., & Holubec, E.J. (1990). *Cooperation in the classroom.* (rev. ed.). Edina, MN: Interaction Book Company.

Jones, V. & Jones, L. (1986). *Comprehensive classroom management: Creating positive learning environments.* Boston, MA: Allyn and Bacon.

Jones, V. & Jones, L. (1995). *Comprehensive classroom management: Creating positive learning environments for all students.* Needham Heights, MA: Allyn and Bacon.

Kameenui, E. & Darch, C. (1994). *Classroom management.* White Plains, NY: Merrill.

Paine, S., Radicchi, J., Rosellini, L., Deutchman, L., & Darch, C. (1983). *Structuring your classroom for academic success.* Champaign, IL: Research Press.

Rhode, G., Jenson, W.R. & Reavis, H.K. (1992). *The tough kid book: Practical classroom management strategies.* Longmont, CO: Sopris West.

Slavin, R.E. (1987). Ability grouping and achievement in elementary schools: A best evidence synthesis. *Review of Educational Research*, 60, 471-479.

Sprick, R, (1981). *The solution book: A guide to classroom discipline.* Chicago, IL: Science Research Associates.

Sprick, R. & Colvin, G. (1993) [Video program]. *Bus discipline: a positive approach.* Eugene, OR: Teaching Strategies.

Sprick, R., Sprick, M., & Garrison, M. (1992). *Foundations: Developing positive schoolwide discipline policies.* Longmont, CO: Sopris West.

Sprick, R., Sprick, M., & Garrison, M. (1993). *Interventions: Collaborative planning for students at risk.* Longmont, CO: Sopris West.

Sugai, G. & Tindal, G. (1993). *Effective school consultation: An interactive approach.* Pacific Grove, CA: Brooks/Cole.

Walker, H., Colvin, G., & Ramsey, E. (1995). *Antisocial behavior in school: Strategies and best practices.* Pacific Grove, CA: Brooks/Cole.

Walker, H., Hops, H., & Greenwood, C.R., (1993). *RECESS: A program for reducing negative-aggressive behavior.* Seattle, WA: Educational Achievement Systems.

Ward, B.A. (1987). Instructional grouping in the classroom (1987). *School Improvement Research Series: Close -Up #2.* Portland, OR: Northwest Regional Educational Library.

Watson, R.S., Poda, J.H., Miller, C.T., Rice, E.S., & West, G. (1990). *Containing crisis: A guide to managing school emergencies.* Bloomington, IN: National Educational Service.

Wolery, M., Bailey, D., & Sugai, G. (1988). *Effective teaching: Principles and procedures of applied behavior analysis with exceptional students.* Boston, MA: Allyn & Bacon.

Other Sopris West Products of Interest

Managing Acting-Out Behavior
A Staff Development Program to Prevent and Manage Acting-Out Behavior
Geoffrey Colvin

Managing Acting-Out Behavior is a powerful staff development program that offers educators an arsenal of specific methods for managing acting-out behavior. Developed and presented by a noted consultant in the area of noncompliant behavior, the program consists of a manual (24 pages) and two videotapes that describe the various stages of acting-out behavior (Tape 1), and provide nonconfrontational strategies to deal with these behaviors (Tape 2).

The program is based on the premise that if teachers are able to recognize acting-out behaviors in the early stages and use corresponding strategies to interrupt this behavior chain, they can not only prevent explosive situations from occurring but also make real progress toward improving student behavior. This video program is an economical way to increase the skills of all school staff, and should be a part of any effective school's professional library.

To order additional copies of
The Effective Elementary Classroom
or the publication described here,
contact Sopris West at:

(800) 547-6747
P.O. Box 1809
Longmont, CO 80502-1809
http://www.sopriswest.com